ISLAM

Volumes in the Religious Traditions of the World Series

Edited by H. Byron Earhart

Religions of Japan *by H. Byron Earhart (published 1984)*
Religions of Africa *by E. Thomas Lawson (published 1984)*
Christianity *by Sandra S. Frankiel (published 1985)*
Religions of China *by Daniel L. Overmyer (published 1986)*
Judaism *by Michael Fishbane (published 1987)*
Buddhism *by Robert C. Lester (published 1987)*
Islam *by Frederick M. Denny (published 1987)*
Native Religions of North America *by Åke Hultkrantz (published 1987)*
Hinduism *by David M. Knipe*

ISLAM

and the Muslim Community

FREDERICK M. DENNY

1817

HARPER & ROW, PUBLISHERS, SAN FRANCISCO
Cambridge, Hagerstown, New York, Philadelphia, Washington
London, Mexico City, São Paulo, Singapore, Sydney

 For information address Harper & Row, Publishers, Inc., 10 East 53rd Street, New York, NY 10022. Published simultaneously in Canada by Fitzhenry & Whiteside, Limited, Toronto.

FIRST EDITION

Designed by Donna Davis.

Library of Congress Cataloging in Publication Data

Denny, Frederick Mathewson.
Islam and the Muslim community.

Bibliography: p.
1. Islam. I. Title.
BP161.2.D464 1987 297 87-45172
ISBN 0-06-061875-2

---

87 88 89 90 91 MPC 10 9 8 7 6 5 4 3 2 1

To Fazlur Rahman

Contents

EDITOR'S FOREWORD

Religious Traditions of the World

One of human history's most fascinating aspects is the richness and variety of its religious traditions—from the earliest times to the present, in every area of the world. The ideal way to learn about all these religions would be to visit the homeland of each—to discuss the scriptures or myths with members of these traditions, explore their shrines and sacred places, view their customs and rituals. Few people have the luxury of leisure and money to take such trips, of course; nor are many prepared to make a systematic study of even those religions that are close at hand. Thus this series of books is a substitute for an around-the-world trip to many different religious traditions: it is an armchair pilgrimage through a number of traditions both distant and different from one another, as well as some situated close to one another in time, space, and religious commitment.

Individual volumes in this series focus on one or more religions, emphasizing the distinctiveness of each tradition while considering it within a comparative context. What links the volumes as a series is a shared concern for religious traditions and a common format for discussing them. Generally, each volume will explore the history of a tradition, interpret it as a unified set of religious beliefs and practices, and give examples of religious careers and typical practices. Individual volumes are self-contained treatments and can be taken up in any sequence. They are introductory, providing interested readers with an overall interpretation of religious traditions without presupposing prior knowledge.

The author of each book combines special knowledge of a religious tradition with considerable experience in teaching and communicating an interpretation of that tradition. This special knowledge includes familiarity with various languages, investigation of religious texts and historical development, and direct contact with the peoples and practices under study. The authors have refined their special knowledge through many years of teaching and writing to frame a general interpretation of the tradition that is responsible to the best-known facts and is readily available to the interested reader.

Let me join with the authors of the series in wishing you an enjoyable and profitable experience in learning about religious traditions of the world.

H. Byron Earhart
Series Editor

Acknowledgments

I am very grateful to Byron Earhart, who invited me to write this book in his series, for his constant encouragement, helpful criticism, and tactfully rendered suggestions for improvement at every stage of the writing. My students in "World Religions–West" at the University of Colorado, Boulder, were subjected to the emerging manuscript over several semesters. Their reactions and ideas have also been beneficial. Neither my editor nor my students are to be held responsible for any errors in fact or interpretation or infelicities of style that remain in this book.

Some of the material for this book was gathered in research visits to Muslim countries over a period of years. Grateful acknowledgment is made to the following agencies and institutions: the National Endowment for the Humanities for a senior fellowship in Egypt in 1976–1977; to the Council on Research and Creative Work of the Graduate School, University of Colorado, Boulder, for two Grants-in-Aid and a Faculty Fellowship for field work in Indonesia in May–June 1980 and for nine months in 1984–1985; to the council for International Exchange of Scholars and the United States Information Service for a Fulbright Islamic Civilization Grant in Indonesia in 1984–1985; to the State Islamic Institute (Institut Agama Islam Negeri) "Sunan Ampel," Surabaya, Indonesia, for sponsoring my 1984–1985 research on Qur'ān recitation and providing much guidance and assistance; and to the Indonesian Institute of Sciences ("L.I.P.I.") for research permission. My 1976–1977 Egypt field work was greatly facilitated by the sponsorship of the Center for Arabic Studies of the American University in Cairo, as well as by the American Research Center in Egypt, which made me an honorary fellow and permitted me to use its library and other resources.

Many individuals have helped me, in one way or other, to write this book. In Egypt, Dr. Galal Nahal generously guided me to the *mawlid* of Sayyid Aḥmad al-Badawī in Tanta in 1976, where he helped me observe the proceedings. The Cairene Qur'ān recitation masters Shaykh Muḥammad Ismā'īl Yusuf al-Ḥamadānī and Shaykh 'Amer Uthman, taught me much about Qur'ān recitation in 1976–1977. During 1980 and in 1984–1985, my Indonesia research was greatly enhanced by the advice and guidance of many persons, but especially by Rector Drs. Marsekan Fatawi, Prof. Dr. H. Mohammed Koesnoe, Dr. H. Rachmat Djatnika, Drs. H. Muhammad Ghufron, Drs. Abd Syakur Thawil, Mr. Achudiat, Drs. H. Syamsudduha, Drs. Bisri Affandi, and Drs. Zein al-Arifien of I.A.I.N. "Sunan Ampel," Surabaya; by Kiai H. M. Bashori Alwi, director of the Institute of Qur'ānic Studies, Singosari, East Java, and his fellow recitation master Kiai H. Achmad Damanhuri, of Malang, who permitted me to observe their instructional techniques and kindly received me into their homes; and by Dr. Yahya Lubis and Dr. A.Y. Hasibuan, University of North Sumatra. My discovery of the Islamic Center of Greater Toledo was made possible by S. Amjad Hussein, M.D., President, who invited me to speak at the dinner commemorating the second anniversary of the building of the new mosque. He and the Center's Imam and Director, Abdel-Moneim Khattab, and other members of the Toledo Muslim community provided much hospitality, information, and insight during my October 1985 visit. The ways in which data from Egypt, Indonesia, and Toledo have been selected and presented for this book are entirely my responsibility, of course.

Special thanks are due to Gladys Bloedow and Vin Reno of the Department of Religious Studies, University of Colorado, Boulder, for their always careful and prompt preparation of the typescript as it emerged in various stages. I am also most grateful to my editors at Harper & Row for their meticulous, imaginative, and good-natured guidance of the manuscript through production.

My wife, Alix, and our son and daughter Josh and Sydney, once again patiently endured the writing of a book in their midst, for which they deserve to be canonized.

Finally, I dedicate this book to my honored teacher, colleague, and friend Fazlur Rahman.

F .M. D.

Historical Chronology of Islam

Dates	Major Cultural and Religious Features
To 610 C.E.	The *Jāhilīya* or "Age of Ignorance" in pre-Islamic Arabia
c. 570	Birth of Muḥammad
c. 595	Marriage of Muḥammad to Khadīja
610	Muḥammad's call to be a prophet and the beginning of the revelations of the Qur'ān
622	The *Hijra* or "emigration" of Muḥammad and his followers from Mecca to Medina, which marked the founding of the *Umma* and the beginning of the Islamic lunar calendar
624	Battle of Badr
630	Muḥammad's conquest of Mecca and the rededication of the *Ka'ba* sanctuary as a purely Islamic worship center
632	Muḥammad's death
632–661	The period of the "Rightly Guided Caliphs" (Abū Bakr, 'Umar, 'Uthmān, and 'Alī) and the great conquests

Dates	Major Cultural and Religious Features
661	The assassination of ʻAlī and the rise of the Umayyad dynasty, which ruled from Damascus until 750
680	The massacre of Ḥusayn and his Shīʻite followers at Karbalā', Iraq
750	Fall of the Umayyads and beginning of the ʻAbbāsid dynasty, which ruled from Baghdad until the Mongol conquest in 1258; the ʻAbbāsid period witnessed the flowering of classical Islamic civilization; a separate Umayyad dynasty continued in Spain
1099	Crusaders conquer Jerusalem
1187	Saladin retakes Jerusalem for Islam at Battle of Hattin
c. 1500–1800	Major Islamic empires flourish : the Ottomans in the west, the Persian Safavids in Iran, and the Mughals in India; Islam gradually comes to dominate in the Malay-Indonesian regions and in parts of Africa
1700s	The rise of the puritanical Wahhābī reform movement in Arabia, with strong influence beyond
1800s	Development of various Muslim reform movements and an increasingly strong pan-Islamic, anti-Western consciousness
1900s	Continued renewal and reform of Islam, with emergence of many nation-states dedicated in various degrees to Islamic principles; Muslims experience challenges of modernity and science

■

CHAPTER I

Introduction: The Islamic Umma—*A Community Defined by a History, a Religious Way, and a Culture*

They were Japanese, about twenty men and women, all dressed in white and standing in straight rows behind a stocky, older man with close-cropped hair. This leader recited the first chapter of the **Qur'ān*** in perfect Arabic with a resonant voice. The setting was Karachi, Pakistan's international airport transit lounge during the **Muslim** pilgrimage season, when believers from all over the world make their way to Mecca, in Arabia. The little group of Japanese Muslims was waiting to board the plane for the final leg of their long journey to Jedda, the Red Sea port of entry for the holy city of Mecca. The Japanese performed their prayers in a small **mosque** in the terminal, near duty free shops and refreshment stands.

Japan does not have many Muslims, of either ethnic Japanese or other descent. But the Japanese Muslims I saw at prayer in Karachi were clearly Japanese—in language, manner, and physical appearance—but they were also something else. That "something else" is a

*Terms defined in the Glossary are printed in boldface where they first appear in text.

special style or pattern of behavior and comportment that sets observant Muslims apart from other people, regardless of ethnic, linguistic, cultural, or racial identity.

This book introduces the distinctive features of **Islam** as a religious tradition, while at the same time providing information on the varieties of Muslim peoples. Islam is a complete way of life embracing beliefs and devotional practices within a larger context of regulated social relations, economic responsibilities and privileges, political ideals, and community loyalties. Muslims inhabit at least two cultural spheres, the one they were born into and nurtured by and the one acquired as Islamic identity. Usually the two are closely connected, as in Muslim communities of long standing in the Middle East, Africa, southern Asia, and Southeast Asia. But the cultures and subcultures of those vast regions also have very distinctive individual elements and characteristics that have been blended with Islamic beliefs, values, and behavior patterns. In regions where Islam is practically nonexistent or a small minority there is a greater contrast between the general culture and what we will come to recognize in this book as Islamic culture. Often, observant Muslims have to make difficult choices in places like America and Europe when it comes to social and family relations, economic behavior, food, clothing (especially for females), and entertainment, because of conflicts between what Islamic teachings prescribe and what the dominant culture considers the norm.

But even in countries like Indonesia with dominant Muslim populations and also great cultural complexity, several variations of Islamic culture operate in relation to other dimensions of national life. On the heavily populated Indonesian island of Java, for example, there are three generally recognized Muslim populations. The largest is the *abangan*, mostly working-class people who combine Javanese folk customs and beliefs with Islam in a syncretistic manner. Next are the *priyayis*, descended from the Old Javanese court bureaucracy—they are Muslim but proud of the indigenous courtly tradition and at home with its symbols and tolerant style. Finally are the *santris*, the Muslim "fundamentalists" who closely follow the Qur'ān and Muhammad's teachings (the **Sunna**) and reject traditional Javanese cultural and religious beliefs and practices they consider to be incompatible with pure Islam. There is much similarity and a strong sense of community between *santri* Muslims of Indonesia and strict Muslims in other regions. In my own travels to Muslim countries in the Middle East, southern and Southeast Asia, I have always been able to sense immediately when I was with *santri* types regardless of their actual nationality, because of their strong orthodox faith and behavior patterns.

The Islamic Religious Way

Writers on Islam have sometimes emphasized the doctrines of the religion to the exclusion of the human contexts in which they are believed and the practices by which they are confirmed and celebrated. The central beliefs and devotional duties of the religion of "submission" (*islām*) to God are easy to learn, in the way that the floorplan of an office building can be clearly comprehended by consulting a blueprint. But once the elementary, external facts have been memorized, Islam as a living reality still remains undiscovered until one begins to perceive how the beliefs and practices are integrated into the fabric of social and personal life in specific cultural contexts. Muslims—those who have "submitted" to God—continually explain to interested outsiders that their religion is a "complete way of life" in which no distinction is made between religious and secular and all things are within the purview of Islamic authority and regulation.

Islam and Christianity have been conspicuously successful in spreading their doctrines among peoples of widely varying cultures and geographic contexts. Among religions of Asian origin, Buddhism has spread far and wide. Islam is the only Abrahamic tradition—like Judaism and Christianity the great Hebrew patriarch figures in its myths, and it is dedicated to belief in and covenant with the one God—that has had a major impact on Asia to the point of becoming dominant in some regions. Islam has maintained a more consistent system of fundamental beliefs and practices than any other world religion, including Judaism. Although there are sectarian divisions in Islam, they arose largely from political differences and do not include, except for minor details, differences in worship and devotional practices.

Because Islam is a religion of law and recognizes no sharp cleavage between religious and secular matters, it views all things as under God's legislation. Not all aspects of life are relevant to ritual, but they all have been assigned value by Islamic law on a scale from "forbidden" through "indifferent" to "obligatory." The holy law is known as **Sharī'a**, from an Arabic word which means "way," such as the way to the water hole. *Sharī'a* does not literally mean "law"; rather, it means God's ordaining of the right way for his faithful creatures, a way that includes actual law. It closely parallels the Jewish concept of Torah.

Muslims are fond of declaring that "humankind has no rights, only duties." This plainspoken conviction is foreign to the thinking of Americans, who are influenced by the Declaration of Independence and the Bill of Rights. But Islamic commitment to the way of submission to the one, sovereign God is not a grim totalitarianism. Muslims insist that the only proper relationship between humans and God is that of slaves to master. But God has created the world for just purposes, and he is both righteous and compassionate. God has given his human creatures freedom, along with other divine attributes such as intelligence, will, and speech.

Service to the Almighty must be a free act, which is then rewarded with responsibility in this world. The person who fears only God is raised above all other, lesser fears and enabled to carry on a free and active life as a **caliph**, or "vicegerent" of God. The duties of Islam, then, are entered upon freely and, in fact, are believed to bring actual freedom over against the slavery of human greed, anxiety, desire for personal status, and other things to which humans are prone as imperfect creatures. For Muslims, being in the service of God is not humiliating in the human sense; it is liberating and fulfilling. This conviction is shared by all three Abrahamic traditions, because of their common concern for a life of worship and obedience under their one true deity.

Islam and History

Muslims are defined not only by a religious way and by the cultural forms in which they live, but also by the historical development out of which they emerged. Just as Jews and Christians find in the understanding of their own history a model for their religious lives, so Muslims see in the understanding of the history of Islam an exemplary model that helps sustain both their personal and communal identities. Life is lived on the historical plane, where God is believed to have revealed his will definitively through prophets, signs, and mighty acts. Change and flow are natural, but people cannot merely fatalistically accept whatever happens; their behavior must be intentional and will involve crucial decisions. Opportunities come and sometimes pass by, never to be repeated. Responsible living requires making hard choices. History in the biblical and Islamic traditions is an irreversible process in which fateful consequences are decided, either in close covenant relationship with God or, perilously, outside of it.

Muslims study their history in order to adjust their present course in conformity with its teachings about God's providential acts. To become a Muslim is to submit to this history and be formed by it. As in Judaism and Christianity, there is also a forward-looking attitude that believes that the goal of history is in God's hands. History thus becomes a way of proceeding in life, suspended between the definitive events of the religious community's original constituting

The Dome of the Rock, Jerusalem. This is the oldest surviving Islamic monument, dating from 691-92 C.E. *Although used as a mosque and sometimes called the "Mosque of 'Umar," the Dome marks the traditional location of Muḥammad's miraculous "Ascension" to Heaven. It also marks the place where the Jewish Temple stood and thus brings together meaningful symbols and historical memories of Jews and Christians, as well as Muslims.*

and development and its ultimate goal, "Judgment Day," when God gathers all people to a final reckoning and holds individuals responsible for their acts.

According to all three Abrahamic religions, revelation in the form of scriptural guidance has come down from God. Although natural life contains certain cycles and patterns of repetition, such as the seasons and the recurring generations of plant, animal, and human life, historical existence is essentially one-directional and "linear" and thus full of novelty and suspense. The cumulative history of the past provides crucial indicators and lessons as well as reassurances. Islamic sacred history contains some of what the Bible also preserves, such as memories of Abraham, Moses, Solomon, Mary, Jesus and other exemplary persons. In all the Abrahamic religions historical events are remembered and interpreted as revelatory of God's Providence and purposes for humankind. The record of Islam's origins and development contains, for Muslims, the wonderful story of the people of God in a language and with persons, events, and places of their own. That history will be reviewed in the next chapter.

The *Umma*

The Islamic community is known as the **Umma**, an ancient Arabic religious communal term that spans the range of religion, shared values, and common concerns. *Umma* sometimes has a cultural meaning, but it does not denote nationality, kinship, or ethnicity, at least in its fully developed meaning as the Muslim community. According to the Qur'ān, every religious community is an *umma*. The Muslim *Umma* is the totality of Muslims in the world at a given time, as well as the sense of shared history of the Islamic venture inherited from the past. This latter sense is similar to the Christian notions of the communion of saints, a "cloud of witnesses" and a "noble army of martyrs," all existing in a mysterious manner both in the historical past and present until the final judgment.

The *Umma* is not any particular Islamic culture, even though it has always exhibited strong Arabic influences. Rather, the *Umma* is the shared and mutually compatible, complementary family of cultures belonging to Muslim peoples in many places. This transcultural Islamic "culture" unites and preserves the *Umma* even as it draws strength and specific qualities from its many distinct, component cultures.

There are important synonyms for *Umma*. One is the Arabic word *jamā'a*, "community" in the sense of dominant group. Related Arabic words from the same root include *jāmi'*, "congregator," "collector," which in conjunction with *masjid* ("mosque") means congregational mosque for the performance of Friday noon worship, which must be performed in congregation. Another word is *ijmā'*, "consensus," which is one of the major sources of Islamic jurisprudence. Its relation to *Umma* can be seen in the famous declaration of Muḥammad, "Indeed my *Umma* shall never agree together on an error." The consensus of the *Umma*, according to that statement, is infallible.

Another major synonym for *Umma* is **Dār al-Islām**, "the abode of submission," meaning the lands and peoples under Islamic law and rule. There is an administrative and legal dimension to this term that *Umma* by itself lacks. The paired opposite of *Dār al-Islām* is *Dār al-Ḥarb*, the "abode of warfare," meaning the non-Muslim lands and peoples. "Warfare" refers both to the presumed quality of such places from the perspective of Muslims (namely, that they lack the security and order of the *Sharī'a* and are therefore lands where everyone is at war with everyone else) and to the necessity for *jihād*—"exertion" in spreading the true faith, an activity that may include armed conflict. It is one thing to force conversion, which the Qur'ān forbids; but it is another to conquer territory in the name of God and—from the Muslim vantage point—for the welfare of peoples who stand to benefit from imposition of the holy law. Religious minorities, especially Judaism and Christianity, have their place under the *Sharī'a* as protected groups, but they are under certain constraints, one of which forbids their members to proselytize.

Islam as Orthoprax Religion

It has been common in recent years for scholars of comparative religion and Islamic studies to characterize religions as either "orthodox" or "orthoprax." Those two terms derive from Greek compound expressions of *ortho* ("correct") plus *dox* ("opinion") or *praxis* ("practice"). All religions, of course, are concerned with both teachings and practices: matters of doctrine, such as concepts, symbols, creeds, and theologies, and matters of action, such as ritual, law, and devotional life. So when we describe a religion as either orthodox or orthoprax, we are describing its particular emphasis.

Judaism and Islam are orthoprax religions to the extent that each places fundamental emphasis on law and the regulation of community life, the Jews according to the Torah, the Muslims according to the *Sharī'a*, parallel institutions based on revelation and interpreted by respected specialist scholars. Christianity, in contrast, is orthodox because it has traditionally placed greater emphasis on belief and its intellectual structuring in creeds, catechisms, and theologies. The antilegalistic bias of Christianity, particularly as enunciated by the apostle Paul in his Epistle to the Romans, led to a much less centrally regulated system of worship and communal life in Christianity, in spite of the mighty and sustained efforts of Catholicism, especially in its Roman form, to impose order on both doctrine and practices. The orthodoxy of Christianity extends also to worship and the common life, but doctrine takes precedence as the main formulation of the experience of revelation. The orthodox Jewish and Islamic traditions are also vitally concerned with correct thinking and clear formulation of belief, but knowing the truth without doing it is vanity. In fact, the truth cannot be merely known, in the sense of being brought into mental awareness; it must be fully "known" through realization in action.

Orthodoxy and orthopraxy are really only analytically distinct from each other, and for that reason should be used only for generalization. In every religion, belief and practice and their community context are integral dimensions of the total system of symbols and actions. Yet it is instructive that Judaism and Islam both lack universally accepted creedal statements while they exhibit remarkable liturgical and legal uniformity within themselves. Christianity has generated various creeds, one of which (the Apostles' Creed) is until today recited by Christians in extremely differing institutional and liturgical contexts: Roman Catholic, Eastern Orthodox, and Protestant.

The Muslim World Today: An Overview

Today, sizable Muslim populations exist in Africa, the Middle East, and central, southern and Southeast Asia; in many of these areas

Muslims constitute a majority of the population. In the West, especially in America, there has long been an assumption that the Islamic world is composed mainly of Arabs, although Turks and Iranians are now generally included too. It is true that Arabic language, history, and culture have played definitive roles in Islamic history (to be reviewed in the following chapter), but Islam is a world religion that rivals, if it does not surpass, Christianity in its ability to spread to highly diverse cultures and regions.

By far the largest national Islamic population is in Indonesia, where approximately 90 percent of the 175 million people are Muslim. The second largest national Islamic population is in Pakistan, with about 97 percent of 94 million; the third is Bangladesh, with 86 percent of 97 million; and the fourth is India, with 12 percent of 730 million. Other large Muslim populations exist in the Soviet Union (around 50 million), and China (which an official Chinese census lists at 13 million, probably much lower than the actual number, which may be as high as 100 million.)

NOTE: 3 of 4 ARE IN S. ASIA

One object of this summary is to illustrate how very widespread and numerous Muslims are in Asia, well outside the Arab, Turkish, and Iranian Middle East. Arabs are people who speak Arabic as their first language and not just those people who live in the Arabian Peninsula. They live in countries throughout the Middle East and North Africa. There are more than 160 million Arabic speakers, of whom well over 90 percent are Muslim. Iran's 43 million people are at least 93 percent Muslim, and Turkey's 50 million are no less than 98 percent Muslim. Similar percentages can be found in most other Middle Eastern and North African countries. Sub-Saharan Africa contains at least 100 million Muslims.

It is difficult to arrive at an accurate figure for the world Muslim population. Estimates range from a very conservative 555 million to a possibly optimistic billion.[1] A perhaps reasonable, conservative estimate is 850 million, out of a global population of 5 billion. Only Christianity claims more adherents, over 1 billion. However, statistical figures of religious populations are hampered by inconsistent measuring tools and lack of agreement on membership criteria.

A very significant factor in current and future Muslim populations is the annual rate of growth. Among the twenty-five fastest growing nations in the world, eleven have majority Muslim populations (e.g., Pakistan, Bangladesh, Saudi Arabia, Syria, Egypt, Iran,

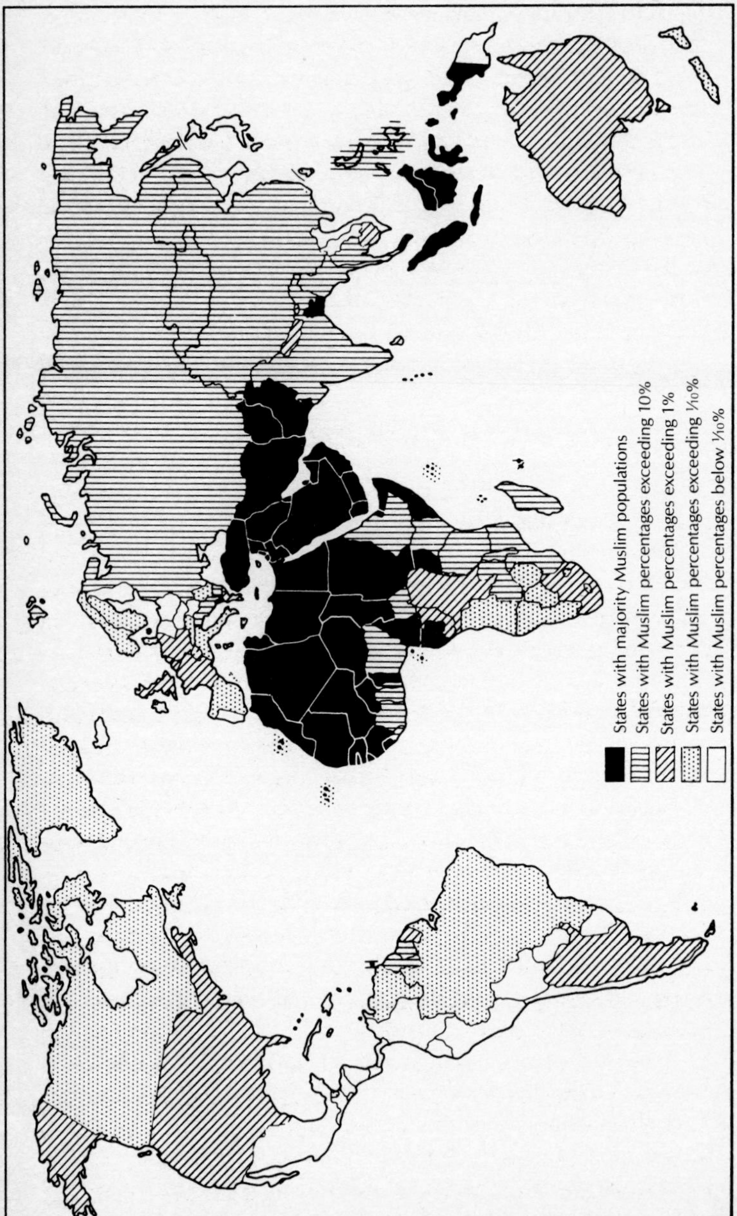

Source: M. Ali Kettani, *Muslim Minorities in the World Today* (London and New York: Mansell, 1986). Reprinted with permission.

Morocco, and Iraq), while others have very substantial minorities (e.g., Nigeria, Tanzania, Niger). Other predominantly Muslim nations, notably Turkey, Chad, and Indonesia, have growth rates well above the world average of 1.7 percent.

For the first time, Islam is becoming a significant minority religion in Western nations, especially France, Britain, West Germany, Canada, and the United States. There has long been a 10 percent Muslim population in Yugoslavia and before religion was outlawed by the Communist regime Albania was almost entirely Muslim. Although most Muslims in the West have roots in traditional Islamic countries, an increasing number are indigenous converts.

Islam as a History, a Religious Way, and a Culture

Islam is a religion marked by a powerful concern for community. The *Umma* may be compared to a triangle with one angle representing history, one angle religious way, and the third angle culture. This triangle can be drawn in many forms, representing the relative prominence of one or another of the three angles. For example, at times and in certain places Muslims have emphasized doctrine and ritual over culture and history, as in some expressions of scriptural **fundamentalism**. At other times, cultural identity within particular regions has been foremost. At still other times, Muslims have emphasized the ideal of certain historical eras of Islam, perhaps in the hope of restoring former strength and glory. But all three dimensions are essential to the *Umma* and exist, finally, as mutually supporting elements of the mysterious reality which Muslims know is their strongest bond: the *Umma* in covenant with God.

Our introduction to Islam as a complete way of life will begin in chapter II with a survey of its rise and historical development. Of central importance in Islam's history is the original and continuing power of Arabic traditions, symbols, personages, moral ideals, and social attitudes. All of these have been maintained through the Arabic language and in the migrations of Arabs. We shall see that, with the coming of Islam into the Arabian Peninsula, old Arabic ways were in some cases rejected, but in others transformed for service in the new religion. At the center of the rise of Islam and inspiring and regulating its continued vitality and development to the present day are the Prophet Muḥammad and the message Muslims believe was divinely revealed to him, the Noble Qur'ān. So, Islamic history has been definitively shaped by its Prophet and Scripture. Muḥammad is thought to be the perfect embodiment of the ideal human life, and the Qur'ān is considered to be a perfect message expressed in the purest Arabic speech, which is believed by Muslims to be the language of God and the angels.

Following our survey of the historical dimension of Islam, we shall examine in chapter III the religion's formal beliefs and practices, which provide the structures of Muslim life. Both aspects have been definitively commanded and regulated by the Qur'ān and the closely associated teachings and example of Muḥammad. The Qur'ān teaches Muslims what God requires of his faithful servants and in the process reveals much of his nature as Creator, Sustainer, Lord, and Judge of the universe. The teaching and example of Muḥammad, known as his Sunna, exemplify the ways in which humans are to receive, ingrain, and apply the message of God. In a real sense, then, the Qur'ān tells humans *what* to believe, and the Sunna instructs them in *how* to believe and act.

The chapter on the doctrines and practices of Islam will go beyond simple description of basics by treating ways in which they have been structured and applied in law, theological reflection, and the interrelated spiritual disciplines known as **Sufism**. We shall see that the sacred law dominates Muslims, especially in its protection and regulation of the all-important communal aspects of life. But intellectual definition and clarification have also been important activities, both in jurisprudence and systematic theology. Even more important, to the point of rivaling the religious law for the loyalties of Muslims, has been Sufism, the mystical path of Islam. Sufism, as we shall see, is personal and spontaneous. It emphasizes love and a warm, intimate relationship with God and with one's fellow Muslims. Sufism has taken on enduring institutional forms in regional as well as international brotherhoods, each with its distinctive emphases in pursuing spiritual enlightenment and mystical union with God.

Finally, Islam is, in addition to being a history and a religious way, a culture. Rather, Muslims constitute a great variety of cultures, all of which conform in one way or other to the ideals and practical requirements of the *Sharī'a*, especially its two most authoritative sources, the Qur'ān and Sunna. There is an Islamic culture that transcends local cultures. In the process, local cultural influences, which always exist, contribute greatly toward making the *Umma* the richly diverse yet spiritually unified community that it is. Throughout this book, attention will be paid to cultural aspects of the *Umma*, whether by describing specific Muslim peoples and their customs or demonstrating the occasional tensions that arise when orthodox-orthoprax Islam is juxtaposed with regional forms and practices, which sometimes include folk beliefs and behavior. In any case, a religion as deeply involved in all aspects of the human condition as Islam is will inevitably have strong cultural dimensions, some of which we will examine in chapter IV, on the dynamics of selected Muslim institutions.

This introduction to Islam closes with a chapter on Islam and Muslims in the modern age. The themes that we shall have come to recognize as being central to the tradition—such as the primacy of the Qur'ān, the exemplary model of Muḥammad as guide for the faithful, Arabic language as both medium of revelation and *Umma*-wide force for community and shared concepts, the *Sharī'a* as God's legislation for Muslims everywhere, and strong Muslim commitment to justice and social order in a harmonious and disciplined community that knows no distinction between "church" and "state," or religious and secular realms—these themes and others will be seen still to inspire and regulate the ways in which today's Muslims believe, behave, interact with others, and anticipate their destinies as servants of God. At bottom, the story of Islam is a story of enduring commitment to a transcendent ideal—God's gracious ordaining of humankind's way on earth and into the hereafter—and the working out in history of that vision.

CHAPTER II

The Rise and Historical Development of Islam

In this chapter, we shall first survey the Arabian setting into which Islam was born, a setting that has continued to exert considerable influence on it to this day. Then we shall survey the major events in the origin and early development of Islam, with special emphasis on the biography of Muḥammad and the role of his key followers who founded the caliphate and established a powerful Islamic international order in the Middle East and North Africa. The spread of Islam to many regions of the world is described next, followed by a consideration of the decline of Muslim political strength as the West rose to global prominence.

Arabia

The Islamic movement arose in Arabia in the seventh century C.E. and declared itself to be a restoration of the original monotheism of the Semitic patriarch Abraham, who was, as the Qur'ān states, a righteous person and a prophet who established the proper worship of God at the **Ka'ba** sanctuary in Mecca. In Islamic teaching, Abraham was neither a Jew nor a Christian, but a person of pure faith and a Muslim (Qur'ān 3:68). The Qur'ān affirms its spiritual pedigree in unmistakable terms: "We believe in God, and that which has been sent down on us, and sent down on Abraham and Ishmael, Isaac and Jacob, and the Tribes, and in that which was given to Moses and Jesus, and the Prophets, of their Lord; we make no division between any of them, and to Him we surrender" (3:85). According to the Qur'ān, the Jews and Christians received true guidance from God and sometimes followed it in a mode of authentic surrender—*islām*—but more often they split up into sects and corrupted the messages of their prophets. Thus God, in his mercy, restored his original message in the Qur'ān, the "Recitation," which he revealed to Muḥammad in plain Arabic speech. Not only the Jews and Christians but also the pagan Arabians descended from Abraham—who had forgotten their true spiritual roots—would be called back to the original religion of Islam, which, according to Islamic doctrine, God had established in archaic times for his faithful servant Abraham and his descendants. To understand the rise and historical development of Islam, we must first look into the region known as Arabia and the beliefs and customs that were followed there before Islam.

"The Arabian Island," as the Arabian Peninsula is known in Arabic, is a vast area approximately equal in size to the United States east of the Mississippi River. Most of it is uninhabited desert similar in appearance to arid regions of Utah, Nevada, and Arizona. However, a minimal amount of moisture and pasture has made it possible for humans to live in parts of Arabia since prehistoric times.

The southern part of the Peninsula, Yemen, was known in biblical times as the Land of Sheba. This region was once a flourishing civilization, with rich agriculture made possible by irrigation, and a complex and interrelated social, political, and religious life that resembled that of Mesopotamian civilizations. The western region of Arabia is rugged and mountainous, with ancient overland north-south routes linking Yemen with Egypt, the Holy Land, and the Mediterranean Sea. Although most of the people of western and central Arabia since early times were pastoralists, by Roman and early Christian times there were also significant permanent settlements, especially in Hijāz, the region in west central Arabia that extends from Mecca in the south to north of Medina.

Hijāz is the cradle of Islam. Before Muḥammad's time, Mecca arose as an important trading town and regional sanctuary and attracted merchants and pilgrims in great numbers. There was, by the sixth century, a growing merchant class that had left behind the old pastoralist way of life. Caravans passed through Mecca going north to Palestine and south to Yemen with valuable cargoes. The close interrelationships between the town and desert Arabs put the Hijāzīs (people of Hijāz), especially those living in Mecca, at a dis-

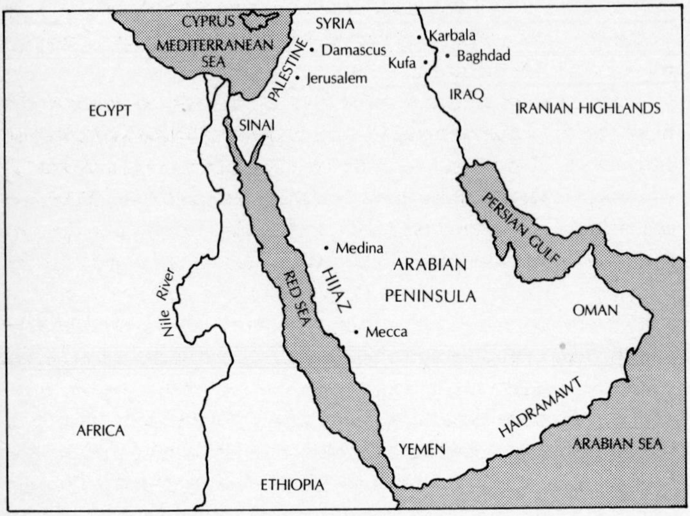

Arabia and the Near East in early Islamic times

tinct advantage in conducting long-distance trade. The camel drivers, rough men with great fighting skills, were masters of the trade routes: they were capable of passing through inhospitable territories by using sheer force or tactical finesse. When necessary, clever merchants could forge alliances and treaties with tribes along the routes, guaranteeing safe passage and shared profits. Outsiders (i.e., non-Arabs) did not stand a chance in Hijāz business or warfare, because they lacked both the camel-based techniques of long-distance transport and the crucially important kinship and cultural ties that united specific Arab groups in closed communities. Outsiders had to have the cooperation and protection of Arabs to be successful.

Before Muḥammad's revolutionary impact on Arabia, it had never known any kind of political unity. The most that had been achieved were temporary federations for specific purposes, such as mutual defense. Now and then a strong leader dominated a limited region, but there was no form of large-scale political unity. Certain essential ingredients for unity were present, such as a common Arabic language, similar social structure and customs, common traditions (especially pertaining to Abraham as father of the Arabs), and mastery of the difficult mode of life in desert and steppe regions, but these were not marshalled in the service of any kind of political unity before Muḥammad.

Before the rise of Islam, the values of the Arabs centered in the honor of the family, clan, and tribe, honor that was to be defended at all costs. This honor was maintained within a context of manliness that expressed itself in martial skills and acts of valor. Manliness was also a kind of nobility of character, evidenced in hospitality and generosity. It was a combination of physical strength, moral courage, and a sense of one's own genealogical superiority. Another characteristic that some Arabs had was known as *jahl.* This term literally means "ignorance," but its connotation is "barbarism," especially in performing violent and cruel acts against others with no motive except delight in wreaking havoc. Barbarism could be overlooked or at least forgiven in a young and impetuous man, because it might be an early sign of unusual potential as a fighter and leader. But if a person's life were continuously characterized by unreasoning violence and wanton destruction, he became a threat to society and had to be subdued or eliminated. Because there was so much lawlessness and violence in pre-Islamic Arabia as well as the absence of a strong religious ethic, later Islamic generations came to call the period before the rise of Islam **Jāhilīya**, the "Age of Barbarism," when people were ignorant of the peace and blessings of true religion.

Pre-Islamic Arabia did have a loose tradition of religious beliefs and practices. In fact, Mecca's central sanctuary housed some 360 idols representing the spirits and divinities found in Hijāz. Chief among them was an image in human form representing the god Hubal, who seems to have had some relation to Mars, the war god. Three "Daughters of **Allāh**" were also worshiped, called Al-Lāt, Manāt, and 'Uzza.

Before the rise of Islam, Arabs also believed in a deity called Allāh, but the pre-Islamic conception of Allāh was significantly different from the notion of Allāh in Islam. Allāh was acknowledged as a creator god, but because he was perceived as transcendent and abstract like the "high gods" of many ancient traditions, the pre-Islamic Allāh was not worshiped formally on a regular basis. The power of Allāh was recognized, and there is evidence that some ancient Arabs focused on him to the exclusion of lesser deities; however, for most Arabs, Allāh was not the center of a monotheistic movement until this was promoted by Muḥammad's prophetic career. Allāh is a contraction of the Arabic definite article *al-,* "the," and *ilāh*, "god"; thus "*al-ilāh*" = "Allāh." Allāh in Islam is the corresponding term for "God" in Judaism and Christianity.

Old Arabian religion recognized the sacred character of places like springs, wells, groves, and unusual rock formations. Often such sanctuaries contained the graves of tribal ancestors, long maintained and guarded as a matter of honor by generations of descendants. The holy character of clan genealogy is apparent in such places. Certain deities had unique relations with particular family and regional shrines, and sacrifices and offerings were made periodically at their altars. This pattern resembles the religious practices of the ancient Israelites as recorded in the Bible, especially those of the patriarchs Abraham, Isaac, and Jacob.

The ancient Arabs practiced circumambulation of their shrines, especially shrines connected with sacred stones. This walking around a sacred site came to be incorporated into Islamic worship in the ritual during which pilgrims circle the holy *Ka'ba* at Mecca. The pilgrimage to Mecca was an important element in the religion of Hijāz long before Muḥammad's time. Pilgrims to Mecca presented many opportunities for trade and commerce and, many Meccan families became wealthy just from the concessions that served the pilgrimage. The close alliance between commerce and religion was a key ingredient in Mecca's prestige and power as the dominant city of western Arabia at the time of Muḥammad. When Muḥammad preached the end of idolatry in Mecca, the leaders there saw him as a real threat to their livelihoods.

We do not know as much about the details of pre-Islamic religion in Hijāz as we would wish. We do know that fatalism characterized much of the people's outlook on life. There was no belief in an afterlife, in a just recompense after suffering, or in punishment after sinning in this life. The ultimate power appears not to have been a specific deity, but rather "Time," an impersonal and indifferent process of change that rolls on despite humankind's hopes or fears. Death was believed to be final, so everyone had to make the most of life now.

There was considerable satisfaction in raising children and in strengthening family size and quality, for in kinship relations were realized the most important goals of wealth, prestige, and power.

Outsiders were not important, because all personal values were in closed community life within the kinship group. Altruistic arrangements were a matter of strict calculation of benefits for one's own group. If someone from one kinship group injured or killed a member of another family, clan, or tribe, there would be a vendetta against the offending kinship group until balance was restored by exacting a life or some equal recompense for the crime. Such feuds could continue for a long time.

The most influential people in ancient Arabia in a religious sense were the *kāhins*, shamanistic seers who could enter a trance state and through visionary means locate lost relatives, camels, or other objects. *Kāhins* uttered sacred formulas in a rhymed prose. Poets were also considered to be repositories of sacred power because of their inspiration, which was thought to be caused by invisible spirits, *jinn* (sing., *jinnī*, from which the English word "genie" derives). Poetic utterance was entertaining as well as edifying. The Arabic language of poetry transcended the dialects of separate tribes and united the widely dispersed Arabs in a remarkable manner at the level of shared symbols, ideas, and aesthetic sensibilities. Poetry was the major art form in *Jāhilīya* times. At the same time, it contained much of historical and descriptive value for the collective memory of the past. Poetic contests were held periodically and the greatest honor was to have one's verses engraved on sheets and hung in the *Ka'ba* sanctuary at Mecca.

Muḥammad: Messenger of God and Founder of the *Umma*

Muḥammad was born in the middle of the sixth century C.E., when Hijāz was enjoying its period of greatest economic progress and growth. A main reason for this prosperity was the diversion of much east-west trade south along the Arabian routes because of a protracted war between the Byzantine and the Sasanid (Persian) empires, the great powers of the age. The lucrative overland trade routes of the Near East and Central Asia were effectively shut down much of the time, so that merchants were forced to look elsewhere for ways to transport goods to and from distant east and west markets and sources. The Arabs had long been preeminent traders, of course, but the impetus brought about by increased use of the Hijāz and other Arabian routes enabled this area, especially Mecca, to become rich.

This development was very influential in the social system, promoting the movement of more and more people to Mecca and changing tribal and clan patterns of mutual support and leadership. The religious dominance of the Meccan sanctuary, especially at pilgrimage time, also generated substantial revenue for those individuals and groups that owned a share in the concessions around the holy *Ka'ba*.

There is evidence that during this period of increased population in towns or even urban settings, the weaker and poorer members of the society suffered neglect. The older tribal system included a loose kind of protection and welfare for less fortunate members such as unmarried or divorced women, widows, orphans, and old persons. But with the shift from rural to urban life the social system deteriorated and social welfare declined. Town and city life tended to produce relative indifference and anonymity. Lucky entrepreneurs were able to make fast money in the caravan trade or in the pilgrimage concessions, but the majority of ordinary folk were left out. Nor was there any widespread religious consciousness of ethical character strong enough to combat the degenerative social and economic effects. Political unity, except in limited contexts, was unknown. It was a matter of people being out for themselves in a highly competitive, heartless race for wealth.

The leading tribe in Mecca was **Quraysh**. Many of its members enjoyed considerable wealth, prestige, and power within the oligarchical system that had arisen in Mecca during the sixth century C.E. The tribe was divided into two major groups, known respectively as the Quraysh of the "inside" and the Quraysh of the "outside." The former were the influential and wealthy members; the latter were people of more humble station. But the tribal system was still strong enough to guarantee that even a "poor cousin" Qurayshī could depend on the strength and dignity of the entire Quraysh tribe for protection if confronted by an outside threat.

Muḥammad's Birth and Early Life

The precise year of Muḥammad's birth is unknown, but it was probably around 570 C.E. Muḥammad's early life was inauspicious—his father died before he was born and his mother died before he was two; he was raised by his loving grandfather who died when the boy was six. From that time Muḥammad's uncle looked after him and continued to provide indispensable tribal protection even when Muḥammad was in his forties and had become a controversial religious reformer.

Muḥammad's clan within the Quraysh tribe was Banū Hāshim, a dignified but less influential or wealthy clan than Banū Umayya, which was chief among the Meccan oligarchy. (The later Umayyad dynasty would rise from that clan and rule the young Islamic empire from Damascus.) Muḥammad grew up a poor orphan and worked as a shepherd in the environs of Mecca. He did benefit from being sent out to live among the desert Bedouin in that it enabled him to learn the pure Arabic language and to become trained in basic techniques of desert travel, survival, and self-defense. Even when many Arabs had settled down in towns and cities, they continued to send their sons off to nomadic tribal relatives for training in the lore and skills of the traditional Arabian way of life, which was considered to be essentially superior to sedentary life on the land.

We do not know much about Muḥammad's youth, except that he developed a reputation as a trustworthy person with unusually good sense about human relationships. In his twenties Muḥammad went to work for Khadīja, a widow who owned a caravan business. Because Muḥammad succeeded so well in helping his employer make a profit and because of his appealing personal qualities, Khadīja proposed marriage, and the two were wed when Muḥammad was about twenty-five and Khadīja perhaps as much as fifteen years older. This marriage provided Muhammad a secure livelihood, because Khadīja was well off and happy to be the source of Muḥammad's good fortune. Several children were born of the marriage, including Fāṭima, the daughter who would become, with her husband, 'Alī, two of the greatest personages of early Islam. During Muḥammad and Khadīja's long and fruitful marriage, which lasted from 595 to 619 C.E. Muḥammad had no other wife. It appears that the marriage was a very strong and satisfying one. Muḥammad had the greatest affection and respect for Khadīja, who did so much to support him during difficult times in his life, especially when he first began receiving his prophetic revelations around 610; at this time he was already forty and she fifty-five.

Muḥammad's Prophetic Career

We do not know much about Muḥammad's life between his marriage to Khadīja and the beginning of his prophetic career, a period of fifteen years. We do know that Muḥammad increasingly took to private religious meditation, including protracted retreats in a mountain cave outside Mecca. Muḥammad's religious practices seem to have had much in common with a wider spiritual movement within Arabian society. During the time Muḥammad lived, other serious and sensitive individuals were seeking a deeper spiritual experience. The name **ḥanīf**, which occurs in the Qur'ān, refers to persons of monotheistic convictions who were neither Jews nor Christians. Abraham is called by the Qur'ān a *ḥanīf* and also a "muslim," that is, one who is submissive to God (3:67). The Qur'ān proclaims that Abraham had established the original ethical monotheism in Arabia, but that it had gradually degenerated after him into the polytheistic idolatry that prevailed in Muḥammad's time. Yet there were still a few persons remaining, as *ḥanīfs*, "rightly inclined" (as the term means) toward the correct way. Muḥammad was among these *ḥanīfs*.

One day when Muḥammad was meditating in a cave on Mt. Hira, a voice declared to him that he was the messenger of God. Muḥammad was frightened by this experience, which was followed by the command "Recite!" Muḥammad said that he could not. After a repetition of the command accompanied by a heavy pressing down on his body by the unknown, mysterious presence, Muḥammad was then told: "Recite! 'In the name of your Lord who created, created humankind from clotted blood.' Recite! 'And your Lord is the most noble, who teaches by the pen, teaches humankind that which they did not know' " (96:1–5). Muḥammad believed that he saw the source of the command to recite as a gigantic figure on the horizon. Muslim tradition has considered that figure to have been the archangel Gabriel, the angel of revelation of the Qur'ān.

Muḥammad hurried to his wife, Khadīja, to tell her of his experience. She received the news in a serious and positive manner and soon became the first to believe and submit to the new revelation as a Muslim. Soon others followed suit, both within the Prophet's family and outside. After a hiatus the revelations continued until the end of Muḥammad's life. Muḥammad sometimes experienced discomfort during the coming of the revelations, but over the years he became accustomed to the visitations of Gabriel. Even so, his receiving of the divine message by means of **waḥy**, a kind of verbal inspiration, was never to be dull routine. The accumulated revelations were known as *qur'āns*, " recitations," both because they were first revealed to Muḥammad in recited form and because they were in turn recited by Muḥammad and his fellow Muslims. The emerging Scripture of Islam was known as the Qur'ān, "The Recitation," the collection of the individual recitations revealed by means of *waḥy*.

The call of Muḥammad to be a prophet occurred in 610 C.E., when he was about forty years of age. In the ensuing years Muḥammad built up a loyal following in Mecca composed mainly of rather humble citizens. The center of the faith that Muḥammad preached by means of the revelations was submission to the one true God, who had spoken before to Abraham, Moses, Jesus, and other prophets known in the biblical record of Judaism and Christianity. The name of the new religion was to be Islam, which means "submission," and one who submits is called a "Muslim."

The early years were relatively calm, enabling the Muslims to develop their characteristic devotional practices centering in a prayer service of several complete prostrations. The emerging Qur'ān was taught to the believers, many of whom memorized it and used it in their own devotions and meditations. The Muslims worshiped at the *Ka'ba*, which they believed was originally dedicated to Allāh by Abraham. As the new movement became more energetic, especially over against the idolatry of the main *Ka'ba* cult, difficulties increased.

Muḥammad's early years of preaching in Mecca constituted a period of gradual growth of the Muslim community, but increasingly Muḥammad came to be at odds with many of the leaders of the Quraysh, who saw in him a potential threat to their economic and religious system. Muḥammad preached against the idolatry of the *Ka'ba* cult, which was a primary source of income in the pilgrimage system. There was also apprehension on the part of the Meccan oligarchs that Muḥammad was a threat to the established social system, which had held the people together since ancient times. It was disrespectful as well as dangerous for Muḥammad to question the ways of the ancestors, whose memory and nobility were preserved in honored genealogical traditions.

As persecution of Muḥammad and his followers became severe, Muḥammad sent a number of Muslims across the Red Sea to the Christian kingdom of Ethiopia. Muḥammad and some of his followers enjoyed the protection of powerful clansmen in Mecca, but other followers did not have such security. Those were the ones who participated in Islam's first *hijra*, or emigration. The Meccan leaders sent a delegation after these Muslim emigrants, committed to return them to Arabia and "submission," not to God, but to the Meccan establishment. The Ethiopian king, however, refused to turn over the religious refugees and gave them hospitality and protection in his realm. But emigration to Ethiopia was not practical for the entire community, nor did Muḥammad want to leave his native land.

Muḥammad realized that the Muslim movement could not continue in Mecca, so he looked around for a new base of operations. He attempted to negotiate with the leaders of the not-too-distant mountain town of Ta'if, but the residents there drove the Prophet away with abuse and stone throwing. This occurred near the end of the first decade of Islam, about 620 C.E. During that critical period Muḥammad's beloved wife, Khadīja, and his uncle and protector, Abū Ṭālib, died.

A delegation from the agricultural oasis town of Yathrib, nearly three hundred miles north of Mecca, met with Muḥammad and asked him to move to Yathrib and serve as arbitrator and counselor to lead that bitterly divided community. Two Arab tribes, the Aws and the Khazraj, were at odds with each other, while the long-standing Jewish community of Yathrib was caught uneasily in between. Muḥammad grasped this opportunity to move his following to Yathrib. He concluded a pact with the delegation, and it was agreed that the Muslims could emigrate with him and that the people of the town would submit to God as Muslims and respect Muḥammad not only as leader but Prophet, that is, God's messenger and guide for the new religion. Although the natives of Yathrib did not immediately become Muslims in the fully devout sense, they did recognize that it was in their interest to give the new arbitration plan a chance for political, economic, and social purposes. An outsider, although not welcome by all parties, could at least claim neutrality.

Muḥammad did not insist that his fellow Muslims move to Yathrib, although almost all of them chose to do so. The emigration was achieved without fanfare, with groups moving north different times, partly to avoid alarm in Mecca. Muḥammad, his close companion, Abū Bakr, and his son-in-law 'Alī were the last to leave. Just before Muḥammad planned to depart, the Meccans attempted to assassinate him while he slept. But the cautious leader had foreseen this and arranged to have 'Alī occupy his bed that night. No harm was done to 'Alī; Muḥammad and Abū Bakr hid in a cave. The patrolling Meccan leaders, thwarted by 'Alī's ruse, also passed by the mouth of the cave. Legend says that a spider web across the entrance made it look unoccupied.

Muḥammad and Abū Bakr traveled to Yathrib by a circuitous route. On reaching the outskirts of the oasis, the emigrants along with the curious natives, gathered to greet their leader. Muḥammad thus had a proper reception, which was to prove auspicious for his and Islam's future success. Yathrib came to be called al-Medīna, "The City," because of Muḥammad's move there. (The full name is Medīnat al-Nabī, "The City of the Prophet.") The **Hijra**, or "Emigration," took place in September of 622 C.E. July 1 of that year came to be the beginning of the Muslim calender[2], because it was with the *ḥijra* that the Muslim *Umma* began.

Several distinct groups came into being as a result of the *Hijra*, both within and outside Islam. Those who made the *Hijra* became known as *Muhājirūn*; they have a special place of honor in Islam. The Medinan supporters of Muḥammad were known as the *Anṣār*, or "helpers." Tradition came to refer to the equivocal or recalcitrant Medinans as *Munāfiqūn*, "hypocrites." Added to these three main groups were the Meccans, who were now the enemy, and the Jews, who occupied a difficult position as monotheists who were skeptical about Muḥammad's religious authority but for a time cooperated and even worshiped alongside the Muslims. Eventually the Jews would be eliminated from Medina, because of a breach caused by their failure to support Muḥammad against an invading Meccan force. The men were executed and the women and children deported.

In Mecca, Muḥammad had organized a religious cult, but in Medina he became political and military leader as well as spiritual guide of a far wider movement. The *Hijra* resulted in the founding of the *Umma*, the Muslim "community," which from that moment has ideally been a union of "church" and state, with no essential distinction between religious and secular life. The revelations of the Qur'ān during the Meccan years emphasized God's absolute unity, sovereign will, justice, and compassion; there was ample warning for humans to repent and submit before an awful judgment would come and divide people into those destined for heaven and those condemned by their wicked ways to hell. Many stories of prophets and their peoples of old were revealed in the Meccan years. In Medina, however, in addition to the themes of judgment and warning, there was much Qur'ānic revelation about communal, ritual, and legal matters. The developing theocracy of the *Umma* needed guidance of a more mundane, practical sort.

The emigrants experienced difficulty finding their niche within the economic life of Medina. They had been traders in Mecca, but Medina was agricultural. Muḥammad organized his fellow emigrants into raiding parties and gained much booty from attacks on Meccan caravans. In 624 (2 *Hijra*), a large Meccan force rode north to protect a homecoming caravan from the Muslim raiders. The two forces, approximately 950 Meccans and 300 Muslims from Medina, met in a bloody battle at the wells of Badr, near Medina. The outnumbered Muslims routed the Meccans and gained an enduring sense that day that God had sent his angels to fight on the side of Muḥammad. This "Day of Discrimination" has remained in Muslim memory and sentiment a providential sign of God's special favor.

Even though the Muslims suffered serious defeats in two later engagements with Meccan punitive expeditions, the *Umma* continued to grow and thrive. Muḥammad as a charismatic prophet succeeded in forging pacts and agreements with a great variety of tribal leaders all over Arabia, so that by 628 he and his followers were strong enough to plan an attack on Mecca. Instead a pilgrimage was substituted and Muḥammad and the Meccans concluded a ten-year truce, which was broken a couple of years later by Mecca. Muḥammad thus mounted another military expedition in 630 but finally relented and simply demanded the evacuation of Mecca and its conversion to Islam from idolatry. Muḥammad entered the city as conqueror without bloodshed. He proceeded to destroy the idols in the *Ka'ba* and rededicated the ancient shrine to Islam.

The main characteristics of Islamic belief and practices were developed largely in the Medinan period. By the time of Muḥammad's death in 632, the ritual and symbolic dimensions of the new religion had incorporated many elements of the Arabian mythic past, as well as specific ritual practices and customs. Certain continuities from the past were considered to be part of Muḥammad's restoration of the primeval Arabian monotheism of Abraham and included aspects, for example, of the later Muslim pilgrimage to Mecca known as the **Ḥajj**.

The Holy Ka'ba in the Grand Mosque, Mecca. The black covering contains Qur'ānic passages embroidered in silver and gold. (Photo used by permission of Abdulaziz A. Sachedina.)

Muḥammad's personal life was filled with drama and people. Of the Prophet's numerous marriages after Khadīja's death, that with the young, vivacious 'A'isha (Abū Bakr's daughter) proved most satisfying. Muḥammad never became personally wealthy, but he did give much to others over the years. His home in Medina was also the site of the main mosque of the community. Muḥammad often had to meet with petitioners there as well as judge disputes, just as Moses had done in the Sinai wilderness. The Qur'ān draws parallels between the two prophets.

Muḥammad's great political acumen enabled him to extend the prestige of the *Umma* throughout Arabia by the time of his death. Not all tribes that concluded agreements with him or submitted to his power actually became Muslims at the time, but Muḥammad did require that all who entered into covenants with him pay the **Zakāt**, or "poor tax." According to old Arabian custom, all pacts were automatically dissolved on the death of a great leader. What was different about the *Umma* was that the pact was essentially between the parties and God, who is eternal; therefore the pact was permanent. After the death of Muḥammad the outlying tribes especially had to be convinced of the enduring nature of the agreements they had prudently, if sometimes hastily, made with the Arabian

Prophet. The wars of apostasy, known as the *Ridda*, which broke out in Arabia after the Prophet's death, restored and strengthened the incomplete Arabian unity first achieved by Muḥammad based on a single idea of governance and belief. That is, Muḥammad's successors compelled recalcitrant groups to return to Islam and the *Umma*. Much of the old tribal system continued into Islamic times—and still does—but faith rather than blood relation became the uniting principle of the *Umma* and has remained so on a global scale until today.

The Caliphate

The Rightly Guided Caliphs: Abū Bakr, 'Umar, 'Uthmān, and 'Alī

Muḥammad's closest and staunchest companions moved quickly after his death to ensure a smooth and stable succession. Abū Bakr, one of the chief converts from the Meccan days, was selected by a small group to be *khalīfa* ("Caliph"), or "deputy," of the Prophet. The caliphal position was political and military, but not religious, at least in the sense that Muḥammad had been a religious authority. Muḥammad was declared by the Qur'ānic revelation to be the "Seal" of prophecy, which means both the final prophet and the validation of earlier prophets from Adam through Jesus.

Abū Bakr ruled during a brief but critically important period from 632 to 634 when many groups had pulled away from the *Umma*. He presided over the struggles that brought the Arabs back into the Islamic fold. His successor was the redoubtable 'Umar, one of the greatest additions to the Muslim cause during late Meccan times, who as Caliph masterminded and led the great Arab-Islamic conquests in Palestine, Syria, Egypt, North Africa, Iraq, and the Iranian highlands and beyond. 'Umar was the first Caliph to bear the title "Commander of the Faithful." He was both respected and feared. His personal integrity was legendary and his frugality extreme. 'Umar ruled an ever-increasing territory until he was killed by a servant in 644.

Abū Bakr and 'Umar and others who had been at the Prophet's side from Meccan times comprised a sort of Islamic aristocracy, distinguished from the Qurayshī elite of wealthy and influential individuals like the Banū Umayya. After 'Umar's untimely death, the Muslim leaders settled on a compromise candidate, 'Uthmān. 'Uthmān was a member of the Banū Umayya clan and the only representative of the Meccan oligarchy to have converted to Islam during the difficult Meccan years. He was a pious and personally upright man, but as Caliph he earned the censure and disrespect of many by his weakness and nepotism. His major achievement was the commissioning of a group of experts to collect all the known copies and variants of the Qur'ān and establish a standard text, which would be used by all Muslims. 'Uthmān came to a tragic end when dissidents stormed his residence in Medina and killed him even while he was holding the Qur'ān. The killing of 'Uthmān would prove a sore point in many future events of the Islamic community, dividing the Muslims politically and spiritually.

'Uthmān's successor and the last of the line of so-called "rightly guided" Caliphs was 'Alī ibn Abī Ṭālib, who was both cousin and son-in-law of Muḥammad and thus a member of "The People of the House," as the Prophet's exalted family were called. 'Alī became leader of a significant faction called the **Shī'a**, which literally means "party." 'Alī and his followers (called Shī'ites) claimed that Muḥammad, before he died, had designated 'Alī as his rightful successor. As it turned out, the majority of Muslims (who would later be called **Sunnīs**) rejected this claim. 'Alī, however, had felt frustrated each time a new Caliph was chosen instead of him. In 656, upon 'Uthmān's death, he finally came into his own as Caliph. By that time, the spread of Islamic power and peoples had reached to distant Khurasan in eastern Iran and Afghanistan. The entire Fertile Crescent and the nearer reaches of North Africa were also part of the *Dār al-Islām*. 'Alī moved the capital from Medina to Kufa, a new garrison settlement at the desert's edge near the Euphrates River in Iraq. This was a more central location, making possible swift communications with the new Muslim provinces east and west.

However, 'Alī's rule was filled with problems. Although he appears not to have instigated or even condoned the killing of 'Uthmān, neither did he punish the guilty party after he ascended to the caliphate. The still powerful and perennially proud Umayya clan (of which 'Uthmān had been a member) resisted 'Alī's rule and ultimately brought it to an end. Mu'āwiya, nephew of 'Uthmān, who had been installed in Damascus as governor of Syria by the great 'Umar, challenged 'Alī's right to the caliphate. 'Alī's and Mu'āwiya's armies met at Siffin on the upper Euphrates in 657. After Protracted skirmishing and fruitless negotiations, the

Umayyad side, prompted by the conqueror of Egypt, 'Amr ibn al-'As, raised Qur'ān pages on their spears and called for a deliberation in which God would decide the matter of who should rule. 'Alī agreed against the wishes of his staunchest supporters. The deliberation, conducted by respected experts on both sides—but with the partisan 'Amr arguing the case for Mu'āwiya—resulted in a decision against 'Alī. 'Alī rejected the unfavorable decision, but he had made the mistake of agreeing to arbitration in the first place. After three more years of attempting to rule a thoroughly fractious *Umma* split between Umayyads and Shīites, 'Alī was finally assassinated by a rebellious member of the new Khārijite faction in 661.

The "Arab Kingdom" of the Umayyads, 661-750

Mu'āwiya became the first Caliph of the Umayyad dynasty, which ruled about ninety years from its capital in Damascus. The old Qurayshī aristocracy was now in control of the political fortunes of the *Umma*. The humiliation of 'Uthmān's assassination was somewhat relieved, although the deed would continue to rankle for generations. Opponents and successors of the Umayyad dynasty derisively referred to it as the "Arab Kingdom," with the word "Arab" signifying ethnic particularism and old *Jāhilīya* habits and "Kingdom" symbolizing haughtiness and worldliness (because God alone is true king of the *Umma*).

Despite such criticism, the Umayyads succeeded in building a powerful state apparatus. They were, for the greater part, responsible Muslims who took seriously the duty to declare holy war against the Christian Byzantine empire, with its capital in Constantinople. The Umayyads also greatly extended the borders of the Islamic world, across North Africa and through Spain into France in the west, and to the Indus and as far north as the Jaxartes River in south and central Asia.

Damascus did not turn out to be the best center for the expanding Islamic empire, although it was certainly central, given the extent of the domains east and west. As mentioned, 'Alī had moved his government to Iraq, and his followers continued to be active there and farther east in the Iranian highlands and Khurasan. In 680, when the Umayyad Caliph Mu'āwiya died, his son Yazīd ascended the throne. But in Iraq a movement favoring Ḥusayn, the son of ʿAlī, gained strength. The Iraqi Arabs resented Syrian rule and they persuaded others in their region to support the grandson of the Prophet. Ḥusayn and his family and some loyal Shīʿites (those loyal to ʿAlī and his line as true Caliphs) traveled to Iraq to join with the movement there, but they were intercepted by stronger caliphal forces and Ḥusayn and his men were annihilated at **Karbalāʾ**, northwest of Kufa. The tragedy occurred on the tenth of the Muslim month of *Muḥarram*, a traditional day of fasting, which ever since has been the Shīʿite day of mourning for its blessed martyrs. The Shīʿite movement, favoring a Caliph descended from the Prophet's family through ʿAlī and Fāṭima, has ever since the Karbalāʾ disaster had a tragic cast in its worldview in which redemptive suffering is a major theme. Shīʿite hagiography later elevated Ḥusayn to restorer of the original Islam of his grandfather, sinless intercessor for his people, and infallible guide **(imām).**

The International Islamic Order of the ʿAbbāsids

The Umayyads ruled until 750, when a Shīʿite inspired revolution toppled the Damascus caliphate and installed a new dynasty in Iraq known as the **ʿAbbāsids**, after ʿAbbās, the father of the first ʿAbbāsid Caliph ʿAbd Allāh. The ʿAbbāsids came to power proclaiming a new order of egalitarianism and brotherhood based on the old Medinan community of Muḥammad and the "rightly guided" Caliphs. By 750 the *Umma* was composed of many different ethnic, linguistic, and cultural groups that had gradually converted to Islam. During Umayyad times Islam was largely an Arab affair. But the religion could not be ethnically contained, for spiritual as well as material reasons. To be a Muslim brought privileges and status. At first, non-Arabs became Muslims by becoming attached to an Arab tribe as a client. Soon there were many clients who provided ready recruits for the revolution against the Umayyads. After the ʿAbbāsids had been in power for a short time, however, they began to behave like pre-Islamic oriental despots in traditional Mesopotamia, whether of Babylonian, Assyrian, or Persian times.

During the ʿAbbāsid centuries, from 750 until the Mongols brought the dynasty to a decisive end in 1258 with the destruction of Baghdad, the greatest accomplishments of Islamic civilization were achieved. Art and architecture flourished, as did crafts, trade, military tactics, and strategy. Scholars made great strides in mathematics, medicine, geography, astronomy, philosophy, and the systematic study of languages—especially Arabic, because it is the language of Qur'ānic revelation. The religious sciences of law, theology, Qur'ānic exegesis, and scholarly criticism of Prophetic traditions **(ḥadīth)** came to maturity in the ninth and tenth centuries.

New waves of people came to dominate in the central 'Abbāsid territories, especially Turkish groups that had migrated from the steppes and mountains of inner Asia. In Baghdad, a round, fortified city built early in the dynasty's history on the Tigris, the Caliphs declined in actual political and military power from about 900, although they continued until the end to wield immense symbolic and moral influence. Practical affairs of state and warfare were in the hands of strong men, who took such titles as *amīr*, "commander," and *sulṭān*, "ruler."

The caliphate provided at least symbolic unity for the vast Muslim domains of 'Abbāsid times. As early as the first century of 'Abbāsid rule, however, an independent Umayyad dynasty was established in Spain by the sole remaining member of the royal family, 'Abdul Raḥmān. Spain developed a brilliant Islamic civilization of its own, with arts, commerce, sciences, letters, and religious scholarship that did not suffer in comparison with the central Islamic lands from Egypt to Afghanistan. Muslims remained in Spain, known in Arabic as al-Andalus (Andalusia), for nearly eight centuries, although their political dominance declined steadily from around the eleventh century, when the Umayyad dynasty there ended. In 1492, the remaining Muslims were forcibly ejected from Spain, and the Christian reconquest of the Iberian Peninsula was achieved under Ferdinand and Isabella.

After the invading Mongols' sack of Baghdad in 1258, attempts at restoring the caliphate were made, most notably in Egypt, but the office never regained real power, in spite of attempts to assume it by occasional strong men down to recent times. It is a tribute to the integrity of the *Umma* that the title "Caliph" could not be easily assumed. Over the centuries, certain prerequisites had come to be accepted for the office, not the least of which was Qurayshī descent. The sacredness of the position of Caliph seemed to increase with its political weakening. As recently as the post–World War I period, a "khilafatist" (from *khilāfa*, "caliphate") movement was active in the Middle East and southern Asia, but the final disestablishment of what was left of the caliphate under the Ottomans by the new Turkish and westernizing dictator Mustafa Kemal Ataturk (1881–1938) dashed the khilafatists' last hopes.

The spread of Islamic political power and the development of an international civilization were not the achievements solely of the mainline Caliphs introduced above. Islamic rulers and thinkers, traders and artisans succeeded in many other places as well. Tenth-century Egypt was the arena for the development of a remarkable Shī'ite caliphate, the Fāṭimids, which was quite independent from Baghdad. The Fāṭimids (named after the Prophet's daughter, Fāṭima, who married 'Alī) founded Cairo in 969 and later established the Azhar University, the *Umma*'s greatest center of religious learning down to the present. Islamic empires arose in Iran, central Asia, Southeast Asia, and the Indian subcontinent. The Turkish Ottoman Empire came to greatness in the fifteenth century and succeeded in dominating not only the Arabic-speaking countries of the Near East and North Africa, but also the Black Sea lands, southeastern Europe, and the Danube territories to the doorstep of Vienna. Farther east, a great Persian Shī'ite empire was established under the Safavids, while in the subcontinent Bābūr founded the Mughal dynasty, which would rule India until the early eighteenth century.

The Ways in Which Islam Spread

There is a long-lived myth that the great Arab conquests spread Islam by the sword throughout the Near East and North Africa. The conquests in fact were not primarily religious, but economic and political, enabling the newly united Arab tribes to continue their momentum as a politically and economically feasible community. Religious faith was certainly the most important element in uniting the varied Arab tribes in the grand venture upon which they engaged. But in the early conquests, there was a clear distinction made between the Muslim Arabs and the subject peoples. Only gradually did non-Arabs embrace Islam, and for a variety of reasons, not the least being a share in the benefits of the Islamic empire. Christians, Jews, and other religious communities with a Scripture—"People of the Book" as the Qur'ān calls them—were accorded "protected" status and required to pay a poll tax. The tax was levied in return for protection and government. Muslims did not pay it, because they already had to pay the religious tax, *Zakāt*, which is a specified proportion of various forms of property.

Within Arabia, particularly, conversion to Islam was forced on idolaters, but not on People of the Book. Motivated more by national pride, even fanaticism, than by fear of annihilation, pagan Arabs flocked to Islam. This strong group feeling, known as *'asabīya*, was known long before Islam on the clan and tribal levels. But it was not until Muḥammad and the Qur'ān came along that a faith and identity strong enough to transcend kinship and regional particularities enabled the Arabs to coalesce into a nation, in fact an *umma 'Arabīya*, "Arabian Community."

Throughout the Near East and North Africa, conversion was generally a voluntary affair, but at times non-Muslims suffered persecution, discrimination, and other indignities. Gradually the Christian communities diminished in size and vigor in countries where they had been strong before Islam. In sub-Saharan Africa, Islam entered through Ethiopia and the Sudan in the east and from the Berber regions in North Africa in the west. Trade was an important means of Islam's spread, but military conquest was also significant. In the subcontinent of India, Muslim military invasion from early times was important in spreading Islam and converting Hindus. But force was not always used. Immigration of Muslims from the northwest added many Muslims to the population, as did the conversion of Hindus. Southeast Asia, the lands which today comprise Malaysia, Indonesia, and Brunei, began to convert to Islam at least by the twelfth and thirteenth centuries, when Marco Polo passed through north Sumatra and reported Muslim towns there. From Sumatra, Islam spread across the Straits of Malacca to the Malay Peninsula, and then down to the north coast of Java. Merchants and traders of mystical Islamic bent were most prominent in spreading Islam peacefully throughout the Malay-Indonesian archipelago, so that today half of Malaysia, virtually all of Brunei, and 90 percent of Indonesia are Muslim. There are also sizable Muslim populations in the southern Philippines and in southern Thailand.

In this century, Islamic missionary activities and the migration of Muslims from the Middle East and southern Asia, especially, have brought Islam to Western Europe and the Americas.

Muslim Political Weakening and the Rise of the West

International Islamic political power reached its height during the fifteenth through the seventeenth centuries, when the Ottoman Turks, the Iranian Safavids, and the Indian Mughals ruled vast empires stretching from North Africa to Bengal. But that period saw also the rapid accumulation of political and economic power in Europe, especially in connection with the development of new trade routes around Africa and across the Atlantic and Pacific oceans. Western nations, especially Britain, France, and the Netherlands, colonized and exploited extensive Muslim territories in North Africa, India, and Southeast Asia. By the nineteenth century, the Ottoman Empire was retreating from its eastern European enclaves and effectively giving up real power in some of its Middle East countries such as Egypt, Libya, Tunisia, and Algeria. The Anatolian Peninsula was the last outpost of the Ottoman Empire, but it was transformed into the modern nation-state of Turkey after World War I and was never colonized. Turkey has continued to be staunchly Muslim.

During this century, European colonialism has nearly disappeared from the world, but the effects of it are still apparent. However, as early as the late eighteenth century, significant Muslim reform movements arose in Egypt, Arabia, and India that started the slow process of winning back Muslims' sense of confidence and ability to govern themselves. The aftermath of World War II included the independence of many Islamic countries all over Eurasia, Africa, and the Indonesian archipelago. In predominantly Muslim countries such as Pakistan, Bangladesh, Egypt, Indonesia, Iran, and Algeria independence in the political sense has been closely associated with strong Islamic faith and practice. The old Islamic triumphalist and success attitudes have returned in strength and, more than satisfying Muslims' desires to live independent of outside control, have increasingly found expression in vigorous missionary activities both at home and abroad, especially in non-Muslim regions. These and related matters will be treated in chapter V.

■

CHAPTER III

The Structures of Muslim Life

Important as the basic elements of the history of Islam's rise and development are for historical analysis and interpretation, they do not provide an adequate sense of what the structures of Muslim belief and life are for the believers. In this chapter, we will consider the basic "story" of Islam from an Islamic viewpoint and the claims the religion makes about the human condition and the ways in which it seeks to realize them at the individual and communal levels.

The Central "Story" of Islam: Good News and Warning

Muḥammad is the centrally important human figure in the drama of Islam's rise and early development into a comprehensive and successful system of religious beliefs, devotional practices, and community ordering. But Muḥammad is not the basic cause of Islam's coming into the world. That fundamental cause is the conviction among his people that God was entering definitively into the Arabian scene and commanding their attention in novel ways.

The Arabic Qur'ān, that remarkable collection of recitations revealed to Muḥammad, was collected after the Prophet's death and circulated among the Muslims in all the places they came to inhabit. This urgent message called the early generations of Muslims to reflect on the old ways of Arabia, so as to realize the chasm between them and the new dispensation of Islamic monotheism. But, more important, the Qur'ān continues to command and instruct people in the present as it challenges them to consider their futures as obedient servants of God.

The story of Islam as understood by Muslims is grounded in the Qur'ān. The Qur'ān teaches that God created the heavens and the earth, that he is One and untouched by his creation, that his angels carry out his decisions and communicate with humans through prophetic inspiration. God has entrusted prophets of old with his message of justice, mercy, and a final judgment, with salvation in paradise for believers and fiery damnation in hell for infidels. God's justice, tempered by compassion, requires that he communicate this message to all people. The Arabs were the last human community to receive the message, and through their tranformation into the Muslim community they were entrusted with the task of calling all people to Islam. The Qur'ān calls the Muslim community, the *Umma*—which in the time of its revelation meant the Arabian monotheists who followed Muḥammad's way—a "mid-most community," marked by balanced moderation and awareness of its responsibility to serve as the model for the Muslim community in its ever-expanding future development beyond Arabia.

The Qur'ān often calls people to reflect on God's providential signs: in the natural world, in the seasonal round of plant and animal life and the regular courses of the heavenly bodies; and in history, in the wonderful deliverances of upright people and the deserved punishment of wayward folk in the Arab, Jewish, and Christian traditions. A recurrent theme is humans' ingratitude for the blessings they have received. The Qur'ānic term for "infidel" is actually shaded more toward meaning one who lacks thankfulness, rather than one who disbelieves. There is something fundamentally wrong with a person who fails to acknowledge with wonder and gratitude all that he or she has received without effort or asking. Such a person ignores, or, as the Qur'ān says, "covers" or "hides" God's blessings and thus fails to enjoy the close linkage with the Creator that is his or her birthright.

At the core of this notion of gratitude versus ingratitude is the Qur'ānic good news that humans have been created with a sound nature and provided by God with a true religion that enables them to have fullness of life through close communion with God in this world and the next. Each human is a religiously grounded person, created and endowed with a **fiṭra**, a "sound constitution" that acts as a kind of internal guidance system and way to God. That is our "natural" birthright. But humans also are cultural beings, in that God has permitted, indeed commanded, them to participate in the creation of meaning in this life and to be lords over all other aspects of creation. The Qur'ānic word for such a human "lord" is "caliph," which means "deputy" or " "vicegerent" of God on earth. The religio-political rulers of the Islamic empire in its first centuries thus received their title of "caliph" from the Qur'ān. They and their institution failed in the long run, but the notion of God's caliphate has persisted, with its deepest meaning being each Muslim's own commitment to ruling for God in this life by means of the opportunities that are available and through the abilities and knowledge one has been granted.

Mystically inclined Muslims have always been held captive by a saying Muḥammad attributed to divine inspiration that God was a "Hidden Treasure," who wanted to be known and so he created the world of sentient beings for community with himself. We humans, according to this story, are endowed with the divine nature to the extent that God is pleased to contemplate himself through our own being and devotion, in a kind of mirroring of his glory and goodness.

To be satisfied with our lower selves and to stray from what God has provided in the way of our natural capacities, on the one side, and from our privileged access to revelation in the form of the Qur'ān and the Scriptures that preceded it, on the other, is to be guilty of both moral and intellectual error. Islam provides the way back to God, through a vital process of living in this world in God's presence by means of faith, obedience, and abiding hope. If we persist in our individual, straying paths, satisfied with ourselves and blinded by feelings of self-sufficiency, we shall, the Qur'ān warns, be doomed.

In summary, the Qur'ān provides the good news of what we are, where we came from, and where we are bidden to go as faithful servants of God. But the Qur'ān also warns us of the "awful journey's end" for those who fail to return by repentance to the "Straight Path" of submission and faith—whether by outright refusal by hardness of heart and opaqueness of reasoning or by placing our individual egos ahead of God's service. To reject God is to reject our true nature and to refuse to realize our true nature, our *fiṭra*, is to be astray and bound for loss. We cannot destroy our *fiṭra*, but we can fail to be saved by it, because God has provided along with it the freedom for us to imagine and to choose. Free will, not fatalism, is at the heart of Islam's teaching about the human condition; but this freedom is not license nor is it by itself a guarantee of success. Rather, free will is its necessary condition, whereas God's will and power and compassionate relenting are its final cause.

The Goal of Islam: "Success" in This World and the Next

Most religions have some sort of doctrine of salvation, in the sense that they envision the possibility of attaining a better state than the one that comes about in the normal, this-worldly course of events. Of course the word "salvation" is not universal, but the concept is found in most traditions. However, the term "salvation" is native to Islam. For example, it may mean a literal deliverance, as when the Qur'ān tells of Jonah having been delivered from the belly of the great fish, a story that it shares with the Bible. But the most characteristic word that Muslims use to express their final religious goal, although it is sometimes translated as "salvation" even by Muslims, is best rendered as "success." A typical Qur'ānic definition of this notion is contained in a passage that sets forth the virtue of the revealed Word:

> This is the Scripture whereof there is no doubt, a guidance unto those who ward off evil. Who believe in the unseen, and establish worhip, and spend of that We have bestowed upon them; And who believe in that which is revealed unto thee (Muḥammad) and that which was revealed before thee, and are certain of the Hereafter. These depend on guidance from their Lord. These are the *successful* (2:2–5).

Muslims believe that God alone is able to bring about his servants' success, but the efforts of the Muslims are essential, too. Faith and works both procure God's blessings and reward, but the very faith that uplifts the Muslim is itself God's gracious gift, too.

God saves the repentant sinner who mends her or his ways sincerely, but God will not accept the repentance of one who is at the verge of death. There must have been an established pattern of repentance and good works, even if it was preceded by a life of evil-doing and unbelief. But there is nothing in humans that is essentially—that is, fundamentally and irrevocably—evil. At their core, recall, humans are constituted according to the *fiṭra*. Therefore no doctrine of salvation ever developed in Islam—at least in the dominant Sunnī majority—that required an atoning, or substitutionary, sacrifice in which wayward and sinful humans are "bought back," *redeemed* and rendered acceptable to God through sheer grace, as in Christian salvation doctrine.

Muslims do acknowledge sin and its ravages, but they consider God's guidance in the Qur'ān and his constant presence and goading compassion to be all that humans need to direct them aright, bringing them, because of their good center, back to the truth. Far from being alienated from God, humankind's own thirst for justice and balance, which can be witnessed even among secular, atheistic persons, is testimony to the Divine Justice, which has determined our deeply ethical natures from our creation. Not to recognize the source of our ethical yearnings and convictions is not to display a corrupt nature per se; it is to be guilty of identifying a false ultimate: ourselves or some other aspect of the created world. Recognizing a false ultimate, known by Muslims as **shirk**, is the one unforgivable sin according to the Qur'ān.

The greatest danger to humankind is, thus, *shirk*, idolatrous association of something with God. The Islamic doctrine of *shirk* and its unforgiveableness is a harsh doctrine, to be sure, but in application the doctrine means that a *habitual*, unrelenting pursuit of what the modern Protestant Christian theologian Paul Tillich calls an "idolatrous ultimate concern" carries with it its own death sentence. Idolatry, at bottom, whether it is a credulous worship of an actual graven image or the crazed pursuit of wealth, power, pleasure, or fame is like betting on the wrong horse or investing in a bankrupt cause. *Shirk* is the refusal to recover the divinely appointed and life-giving *fiṭra* in our inmost being. *Shirk* is denying the truth about *ourselves* just as much as it is a literal focus on something other than God. Our lower selves, our greedy and vain feelings of self-sufficiency, are actually not the most real parts of us. To act as if they were is to cut ourselves off from God by denying his ground within us. *Shirk*, then, is not so much a matter leading to God's refusing to forgive us as it is our refusal to acknowledge him. How can he forgive that, and even if he "can," why, in a universe established according to justice *should* he? Do people, who have been invested with intellect enough to conceive of the divine nobility and nature, want to end up with a God who overlooks and in the act ignores our stupidity? Our perverse failure to be our true selves is damnable, Islam argues.

The success that Muslims hope for in this world runs the gamut from ordinary physical and emotional well-being—like Job's blessed existence before his trials: a large, happy family, many cattle, and the admiration and respect of his associates—to more inward states marked by serene joy, steadfast patience, faith in adversity, honest dealing in the face of treachery and defeat, and intelligent regard for the wondrous gifts of this life, be they pleasant or painful. In fact, the greatest success in this life seems for Muslims to be being blessed with the faithful, accepting patience that endures all misfortunes and seeks the final outcome only in God's justice and reward. Success in this sense is itself believed to be proof of God's abiding presence. It is not an obvious kind of worldly good fortune but a kind of spiritual poverty of total resignation to God.

The success of the life to come is eternal and sublime beyond the ability of human words to describe. The Qur'ān speaks of heavenly gardens, with sheltering trees, pure brooks and rivers, beautiful serving maidens, and continual joyful praise of God. But thoughtful Muslims of all periods have also discerned in the vivid Qur'ānic depictions of paradise deeper, symbolic levels that ultimately transcend worldly physical description and the life of the senses.

The Realization of the Goal of Islam in Faithful and Observant Communal Life

Muslims believe that they have been called by God to establish a righteous human political and social order on earth. The only way to live gratefully as God's caliphs is to make full use of what he has bestowed on humankind. The fundamental Islamic doctrine of the divine unity requires a unified human religious community as well. **Tawḥīd** is the Islamic name for this unity. But it is not a matter of mere number, in the sense that one is different from two and three and so forth. Rather, *tawḥīd* means "unification"; it has verbal force. Muslims declare God to be One and reinforce, indeed *embody*, that declaration with strenuous efforts at unity in their doctrinal, ritual-devotional, and communal lives, which are regulated by the Qur'ān and Muḥammad's teaching and example as contained in his Sunna.

Faith

The elements of Islamic faith, known as *īmān*, can be briefly summarized, even though there has never been anything like a universal uniform creed in the sense of a formal statement that Muslims have been required to recite and endorse. The closest thing to such is the **Shahāda**, the "witnessing" both to the unity of God and the messengerhood of Muḥammad. But this two-part utterance does not have sufficient specific detail to be a comprehensive creed; rather it provides a crisp summary of the two vast areas of theological awareness and reflection: God and humankind, the vertical dimension being belief in no god but God and the horizontal dimension being the recognition that Muḥammad has been chosen to be God's messenger on the human historical plane. But nothing is said in the *Shahāda* about the Qur'ān, or about the Last Judgment, or other central elements of Islamic faith.

The first basic doctrine of Islam is the belief in the divine unity, *tawḥīd*. This belief is easy to declare but difficult to understand and apply; indeed, the whole edifice of Muslim religion is dedicated to realizing *tawḥīd*. The second great doctrine is belief in angels as the divinely appointed agents of God's revelatory activity and helpers in myriad other tasks. The third is belief in prophecy and sacred books that have been revealed to prophets in the past and, especially, acceptance of Muḥammad and the Qur'ān as the final "seal" of the cycle of prophecy in history. The fourth belief is in the Last Day, when all the dead will be raised and humankind shall be gathered before the Judgment Seat of God, the righteous to be saved in eternal heavenly bliss and the unbelievers to be cast down guilty into hell. The final doctrine is the Divine Decree and Predestination. Its workings are a mystery to humans, who nevertheless are given sufficient freedom and responsibility to make genuine moral and spiritual decisions.

The Pillars of Islam

In chapter I we considered Islam to be a religion with an emphasis on orthoprax issues; that is, the *acting out* of basic beliefs and attitudes is central. This orthoprax character of Islam can best be seen in the five basic devotional-ritual duties called the **Pillars of Islam**, required of every Muslim; these work together to form a potent inner structure for the *Umma* and at the same time demarcate it from and defend it against outsiders.

Muslims have a strong sense of distinction between themselves and non-Muslims. The universal Islamic greeting *as-salāmu 'alaykum*, "Peace be upon you!" is normally used only between Muslims. It is forbidden for female Muslims to marry outside the faith and male Muslims who do are restricted to monotheistic spouses, and children of such a union are considered Muslim and must be brought up so. The closed community of the *Umma* is not inhospitable to outsiders in the sense of being cold or indifferent to common human needs and problems. Rather, the *Umma* is closed in the sense that it does not permit its members to stray outside the fold and still be considered Muslim.

SHAHĀDA

As far as welcoming outsiders into the fellowship of faith is concerned, the gates are wide open at all times and there is always hearty rejoicing when a person responds to the call of Islam, pronounces the Shahāda, and becomes a brother or sister in the faith. It is necessary only to perform the first pillar of uttering the *Shahāda* ("I bear witness that 'There is no god but God'; I bear witness that 'Muḥammad is the messenger of God.' ") once, with sincere conviction, to become a Muslim.

Once, in a university class on Islam, one of my students was inspired to utter the *Shahāda* in the middle of my lecture. He had evidently been thinking about his potential commitment to Islam for some time, but when he felt the call of God in the classroom, he could not resist. Two Muslim students in the class embraced the student and together the three performed a joyful prayer prostration while the class looked on in surprise, awe, and respect lightened by cheerfulness.

ṢALĀT: WORSHIP

The Pillars of Islam begin with the *Shahāda*, which is both a doctrinal declaration and an act of public witnessing. As soon as this brief confession has been uttered, the appropriate next expression is formal worship, known as **Ṣalāt**. This act of worship is the most frequently performed and pervasive of Islam's devotional duties; it is required five times daily and also at other times such as funerals and eclipses. The *Ṣalāt* is highly formalized and minutely regulated in its precisely observed cycles of spoken formulas and bodily postures. Prescribed in the Qur'ān and developed by Muḥammad for the earliest Muslims, the *Ṣalāt* has bound the *Umma* together across the ages and geographical frontiers of Islam at a more nearly uniform level of performance than the practice of any other world religion. There is no priestly clergy in Islam, so all Muslims must know the *Ṣalāt* and be able to lead it if called upon.

Worshippers prostrating during the Friday Ṣalāt in an overflow congregation at the Masjid Jame in the heart of Kuala Lumpur, Malaysia.

Muslims learn early how to perform the *Ṣalāt* as they are trained to form straight rows behind the *imām*, the prayer leader who serves as a pattern and pacer for the series of standings, bowings, prostrations, and sittings that make up a cycle within the service. All eyes are directed straight ahead, with the heart and mind focused on precisely what is to be done during the service. The entire congregation faces in the direction of Mecca and the sacred *Ka'ba* there. The *Ṣalāt* is observed at dawn, at noon, during the mid-afternoon, just after the sun has set, and in the evening. A prescribed number of cycles is required at each of these times, but each worshiper may also perform additional ones.

A prime prerequisite for performing the *Ṣalāt* is ritual purification for every individual; usually (unless there is major impurity) purification is achieved by means of simple washing of the face, head, ears, mouth, nostrils, hands and arms to the elbows, feet, and ankles, while uttering certain invocations for purity and guidance. However, if the individual has experienced what is considered a major impurity, such as sexual intercourse or contact with foul substances such as pigs or dog saliva, then she or he is obliged to perform a major ablution in the form of a ritualized full bath of the entire body. Purification is of such great importance for Muslims that they constantly distinguish between a pure state and an impure state. This distinction stems from the closed nature of the *Umma* and protects it. Closely associated with purity and avoidance of impurity is the legal division of the world and human actions into the basic categories of permitted and forbidden. Not only is it forbidden to perform the *Ṣalāt* without first becoming purified, it is understood that if one observes the *Ṣalāt* while impure, the performance is invalid. The *Ṣalāt* is both an individual and a communal ritual act that strongly symbolizes the specialness of the Muslim community and sets it apart from profane and impure objects and associations. "Cleanliness is next to godliness" is as pervasive an ideal among Muslims as it has been among pietistic Protestants.

The English word "mosque" is based on an Arabic word (*masjid)* that simply means "place of prostration." A mosque, then, is not primarily a building, but a ritually dedicated space. The exclusive nature of the *Umma* is sometimes symbolized in some countries by forbidding non-Muslims to enter a mosque (e.g., Morocco,

Iran). Even Muslims must leave their shoes at the door and in all ways deport themselves fittingly.

Muslim religious and aesthetic inspiration have come together in two supreme expressions in the art of Qur'ānic Arabic calligraphy and sacred architecture. The mosque as a building has reached heights of symbolic expression in testimony to the divine unity by means of its simplicity, spaciousness, and manner of drawing the eyes, ears, and hearts to meditation on God. Sometimes mosque architecture has symbolized the vision of the garden of the afterlife in heaven, with pillars resembling tree trunks and fountains and pools bubbling and spreading out as cool invigorating streams under the trees and domed heavens of the mosque as a miniature paradise.

The first requisite for a mosque is proper placement: the location should be free from pollution (e.g., not next to a tannery or brewery) and the main prostration area must be situated so that the worshipers face toward Mecca (Indonesian Muslims face west, whereas Syrians face south, and so forth). Mosques always have a niche in the wall that faces Mecca, indicating the proper direction of prayer. The niche may be plain and unadorned or lavishly decorated, but the ritual purpose is unvarying. Next to it is a raised pulpit, with a stairway leading up and a canopy over the top. This pulpit is used whenever a sermon is preached, as at Friday congregational *Ṣalāt*, when Muslims are required to assemble together in a major mosque. The floor must be clean and clutter-free. There are no chairs or benches in mosques; the worshipers perform their services on carpeted or matted floors. Usually there are lamps, a clock, and a library corner with copies of the Qur'ān and other religious books available for study. Adjacent to the worship area is a properly outfitted ablution area, with running water (ideally), toilets, and privacy. Usually there is a minaret next to or atop the mosque, from which the call to prayer is chanted. The minaret, in fact, is a universal symbol of Islam. The word comes from the Arabic word for "lighthouse" and the symbolism is obvious—it guides people to the Straight Path of Islam. The call that comes from this lighthouse is God's summons to righteousness and truth: "God is most great! I bear witness that there is no god but God. I bear witness that Muḥammad is the Messenger of God. Hasten to *Ṣalat*! Hasten to success! God is most great! There is no god but God!"

Interior of the mosque at the tomb of the Prophet Abraham, considered to be the Patriarch of Judaism, Christianity, and Islam; Hebron, West Bank. The niche marking the direction of Mecca is to the left of center, while the stepped pulpit is to the right.

ZAKĀT: ALMSGIVING

The third Pillar of Islam is legal almsgiving, called *Zakāt*. *Zakāt* is a kind of religious tax on certain types of property and wealth, provided a minimum level is already owned. It is believed that *Zakāt* purifies the remaining property for the giver.

This almsgiving is rendered at the end of each year for the support of various people: for poor Muslims, for converts who need help getting on their feet (in many societies, leaving a religious community for another has entailed a radical break, sometimes even social and economic "death"), for Muslim debtors of necessity, for Muslim wayfarers in dire straits, for Muslim prisoners of war, for Muslims engaged in the defense of or propagation of Islam, and for those whose job it is to collect *Zakāt*.

Zakāt is not considered charity. Rather, it is a religious obligation and placed right alongside the *Ṣalāt* as a primary act of service to

God. The *Ṣalāt* strongly symbolizes the total submission of the Muslims to the one, almighty God; the *Zakāt* symbolizes the solid communal-mindedness of the Muslims, who support each other with their wealth and thus increase not only the cohesiveness and security of the *Umma* but also render it purer. The Qur'ān likens the *Zakāt* to a good loan paid to God, which he will repay multifold. God thus enjoins the Muslims to participate with him in sustaining the righteous community of faith. Human caliphal activity is a real responsibility and possibility, exercising stewardship of earth's resources. God has endowed his creatures with wealth, and humankind is asked to return it through works enhancing the community. To support the community by *Zakāt*, then, is to worship God.

ṢAWM: FASTING

Fasting, known to Muslims as **Ṣawm**, the fourth Pillar of Islam, is also prescribed for Muslims for the whole month of Ramaḍān, one of the lunar months of the Muslim calendar lasting either twenty-nine or thirty days. No food, drink, medicine, smoke, or sensual pleasure may be taken from dawn until dark. In the evening it is permitted to eat and enjoy marital relations, and before dawn a meal is eaten to provide sufficient strength for the coming day's activities. The ill, children, the aged, and certain other classes are excused from the fast, although those who can should make it up later.

Ramaḍān is the month in which the Qur'ān first came down upon Muḥammad and it is considered auspicious for other reasons, too. Muslims try to improve their spiritual and ethical lives during this holy month. Evenings are spent in special prayer gatherings in mosques, where cycles of pious exercises are recited, some twenty in all. There is congregational recitation of the Qur'ān, as well as increased individual recitation. Some people observe a retreat during the last ten days of Ramaḍān by residing in the mosque.

Ramaḍān is a time of sober reflection and, depending on the season and region, it can be a difficult discipline. But experienced fasters soon get into the rhythm of the observance and testify to physical as well as spiritual benefits of fasting. One of the major benefits is a shared feeling of common humanity, with differences of rank, status, wealth, and other circumstances that distinguish people from each other minimized. With all the effort that the fast entails, Ramaḍān is not a sad or anxiety-ridden period. Evenings are usually joyful occasions and people strive to be at their best at all times and to be especially aware of the dangers of crossness and hasty, angry words. There may be weariness for some, but there is also keenness of perception and self-scrutiny.

At the close of the Ramaḍān fast comes one of the two canonical festivals of the Muslim year, the "Feast of the Fast-Breaking'," when Muslims send greeting cards to each other, enjoy special foods, and travel to be with family. A special *Ṣalāt* service opens the festival.

THE ḤAJJ: PILGRIMAGE

The fifth and final Pillar of Islam is the pilgrimage, or *Ḥajj*, to Mecca during the special period established for it. This is the only Pillar that is not absolutely obligatory. It is to be performed only if personal, financial, and family circumstances permit. Completing the *Ḥajj* confers on the pilgrim the honorific title *Ḥājjī*, which may then be attached to the person's name for the rest of his or her life.

The *Ṣalāt* is a continuous exercise in worship and communal strengthening, with ritual concentration directed toward Mecca. The *Ḥajj* permits the worshiper to travel in body to the sacred center, where Muslims believe that Adam and Eve lived, where Abraham and his son Ishmael erected the *Ka'ba* as the first house of worship of the One True God, and where Muḥammad often raised up the *Ṣalāt* and led his fellow believers, even when they were persecuted cruelly as they prostrated in prayer and praise. Prostration was ridiculed as craven by the proud pagan Arabs; but it became a new symbol of pride for Muslims in submission before their Lord.

Pilgrims experience the thrill of seeing and hearing and meeting fellow believers of all races and languages and cultures from the corners of the globe. Male pilgrims are required to don a two-piece, white, seamless garment, symbolizing their entry into the ritually pure and consecrated state of **iḥrām**. Women may also wear a white garment that covers their entire body and head, but they are also allowed to wear clean, modest clothing in their national styles. When men wear the *iḥrām* garment and women their national dress, Muslims rejoice at this dual symbolism of Muslim unity and equality alongside creative and rich cultural diversity. The *Umma*, thus, is both strongly focused in its common dedication to God, and it is brilliantly diffuse in its variegated cultural forms, all of which are turned toward the common task, which God commanded in the Qur'ān, of "enjoining the right and forbidding the wrong."

Although Islam knows no rite of passage into the *Umma*, the *Ḥajj* can be compared to a ritual of passage marked by separation from one spiritual status and movement to a higher one. The first step in this separation is formal leave-taking and the writing of one's last will and testament. In Mecca, the dedicated state of *iḥrām* requires abstention from sexual relations, from shaving the beard or cutting one's head or body hair, wearing scent or precious ornaments, hunting animals, and uprooting vegetation. The pilgrim is thus separated from everyday life and placed in a special ritual state, a common feature of rites of passage the world over. The actual time of the pilgrimage rites, in Mecca near the *Ka'ba* and in several locales outside, includes ritual reenactments of primordial spiritual events: pilgrims pray where Abraham prayed; they run in frantic search of water like Hagar did for her defenseless son Ishmael, when they were cast out into the wilderness; they circumambulate the *Ka'ba* seven times on three occasions, just as the monotheistic worshipers of old were believed to do and as Muḥammad prescribed by his example; and they perform a blood sacrifice of consecrated animals in commemoration of Abraham's sacrifice of a ram when God had tested his faith and then released him from the awful command to sacrifice his son (which the Qur'ān identifies as Ishmael).

The climactic event of the *Ḥajj* is a standing ceremony on the Plain of Arafat, several miles from Mecca, near the Mountain of Mercy, where Muḥammad sat astride his camel as he delivered his farewell sermon to the assembled pilgrims in the last year of his life. The standing ceremony begins at noon with a special *Ṣalāt* and continues until sundown. The pilgrims observe a reflective afternoon, seeking God's forgiveness of their sins and resolving to spend the remainder of their lives in renewed and more intense service of God and the Muslims. There may be as many as three million pilgrims gathered in the vast plain for the standing ceremony, ample witness to the great worldwide community of Muslims. If one misses the standing ceremony, for whatever reason, the entire pilgrimage is thus rendered invalid and must be repeated in another annual season. Notice that the standing ceremony focuses on the individual pilgrim's own recommitment, which is renewed in light of the reenactments leading up to it. In ritual studies terminology, this is a "betwixt and between" time when a spiritual transformation and the graduation to the new status occur definitively, the status of *Ḥājjī*.

After the standing ceremony comes the blood sacrifice that extends symbolically back to Abraham. This sacrifice—of sheep, goats, camels, cattle—is of double significance. Not only is it a high point of the pilgrimage, a sort of liturgical release just as it was for Abraham and Ishmael; it is also the one point in the *Ḥajj* when Muslims around the world also participate by means of a Festival *Ṣalāt* and animal sacrifices at home. This observance is known as the Great Feast and with the Feast of Fast-Breaking completes the canonical observances of Muslim festivitiy. The performance of the sacrifice is done by pointing the animal's head toward the *Ka'ba* in Mecca, saying "God is great" and "In the Name of God," and then slitting its throat quickly and cleanly. The blood is thoroughly drained before the meat is butchered, in a way similar to the Jewish practice of koshering meat. Again, this is a kind of ritual separation and believed to render the flesh pure as well as wholesome. The meat is divided into portions, at least in the case of Muslims not on pilgrimage, and usually given to the needy, and to neighbors, with the third portion remaining for the use of the sacrificer and his or her family. Only males may perform the slaughter; females have it done on their behalf by a male relative or special agent.

During the final days of the *Ḥajj* and after the sacrifice, the pilgrims gradually emerge from the state of *iḥrām* by having their hair cut and beard shaved, by donning everyday clothes, and by beginning to focus on the tasks ahead beyond Mecca. Sexual relations are still forbidden until after certain final rites have been completed, like the ritual stoning of the devil and a farewell circumambulation of the *Ka'ba*. If they have not done it before the *Ḥajj*, pilgrims usually try to visit Medina, the City of the Prophet, some 280 miles to the north. Medina, like Mecca, is a forbidden city, open only to Muslims. Although the visit to Medina is not obligatory, it is meritorious and always deeply meaningful, because it provides an opportunity to pay respects at the Prophet Muḥammad's tomb and to visit other holy places nearby in this oasis city where the *Umma* was first organized under the guidance of the Qur'ān and God's Prophet.

Emergence from the pilgrimage, symbolized by the lifting of the requirements of *iḥrām*, departure from Mecca, and being welcomed home by relatives and friends (there is typically a large crowd of greeters at airports and seaports) mark the return to normal life in a new status, which ritual experts call "reincorporation." Not only is the *Ḥājjī* permitted to bear that title before his or her name, but in some places there are additional marks of the new status. In Egypt, for example, it is common for pilgrims to have special *Ḥajj* paintings applied to the exterior walls of their homes. Typically, these paintings depict scenes of the journey—a steamship, airplane, camel, or horse with rider (some traditionalists like to enter Mecca as Muḥammad did, on a mount)—and they always contain a representation of the holy *Ka'ba* and usually also the Prophet's tomb in Medina. Such *Ḥajj* art can be interpreted at various levels, but the main meaning, according to recent field analyses, centers in Egyptian ideas of saintly persons and the blessings and spiritual power that they provide in a community. The returning pilgrim is, as it were, a living saint who resides in a sacred house marked by the symbols of the supreme centers of Islamic sacral power, Mecca and Medina.[3]

JIHĀD

The five Pillars of Islam—witnessing to God's oneness and Muḥammad's messengerhood, worship through the *Ṣalāt* Service, almsgiving, fasting in Ramaḍān, and pilgrimage to Mecca—constitute only a minimum structure of Muslim orthopraxy. There are also many additional practices both at the individual and communal levels that make up the total way of life that is Islam. The Muslim term for worship is **'ibāda**, a word that literally means "service," in the same sense Christians mean it when they say worship "service." God is *served* through worship, and worship is reserved for God alone. One additional form of service to God in Islam is *jihād*, whose meaning must be carefully explained. *Jihād* is often mentioned in news releases from the Middle East in which Muslims have proclaimed "holy war" against evil and Islam's enemies, whether Western countries or fellow Muslims with whom they disagree (the extremist "Islamic Jihad" movement in Lebanon is an example.) But *jihād* properly speaking means "exertion" in the way of God. It may mean fighting against Islam's enemies or even attempts to spread the religion by force (although Muslim opinion on the latter differs sharply); but a famous teaching of Muḥammad's holds that the "greater *jihād*" is the spiritual struggle each individual has with her or his own faith and need for repentance, whereas *jihād* as armed conflict is called the "lesser" exertion. Whatever the prevailing opinion or practice, *jihād* has sometimes been considered a sixth Pillar of Islam, and thus a form of "worship," or "service" according to specified rules.

Guidance for the *Umma* in the Form of Holy Scripture and Prophetic Example

The two-fold structure of the *Shahāda*, focusing first on God's unity and second on Muḥammad's prophetic role as messenger, is embodied within the Muslim community by the Qur'ān, which for Muslims contains God's revealed guidance, and by the Prophet's Sunna, which contains Muḥammad's "custom," as recorded in reports telling of his teachings and actions. These reports are regarded by Muslims as supremely worthy of learning, obeying, and, where appropriate, imitating.

The Qur'ān

The Qur'ān was revealed to Muḥammad by a mysterious process of verbal inspiration, believed to have been mediated by the archangel Gabriel. Muslims insist that the Qur'ān contains only God's words and nothing of human admixture, whether from Muḥammad or from other sources (such as other scriptures, like the Bible). Muḥammad received and transmitted the Qur'ānic recitations as they came down to him. The accumulating body of revelation came early to be used by the Muslims as their prayerbook and source of guidance. In fact, one of the several synonyms for the Qur'ān is "The Guidance." Another is "The Criterion"—between good and evil, truth and falsehood.

After Muḥammad's death, his companions collected the Qur'ānic materials and eventually succeeded in arranging them in written, book form to the satisfaction of the knowledgeable of the day who had been at Muḥammad's side, recited the material with him and other reliable companions, and knew it well. Thus, the Qur'ān, both as live recitation and as book, came into being in the full light of history and was declared valid before a qualified representative grouping of Muslims of the Prophet's circle. That is a remarkable pedigree for a sacred Scripture when compared to other holy books; most holy books tend to emerge from diverse origins and develop gradually into their eventual canonical form.

The complete Qur'ān is almost the length of the Christian New Testament. A chapter is called a **sūra** and there are 114 of them, arranged more or less from longer in the beginning down to shorter ones toward the end. The first *sūra* is a short prayer, which, like the Lord's Prayer of Christianity, stands as the model of prayer for Muslims. It reads, in translation from the original Arabic:

> In the Name of God, the Beneficent, the Merciful.
> Praise Belongs to God, the Lord of all Beings,
> The Beneficent, the Merciful.
> Master of the Day of Judgment,
> You alone we worship, You alone we ask for help.
> Guide us on the straight path,
> The path of those to whom You have been gracious,
> Not of those with whom You are incensed
> Nor those who are straying.[4]

This prayer, known as "The Opening," is uttered in each cycle of the *Ṣalāt* and on many other occasions, too, and is learned very early in a Muslim's life.

The second *sūra*, called "The Cow" because of the occurrence of that word in connection with the story of Moses and the people of Israel, is sometimes also called the "Qur'ān in Miniature," because it contains all the main features of the message and was revealed after the *Hijra* of Muḥammad from Mecca to Medina, when the main elements of the religion had been established. Certain passages dealing mainly with legislative matters are from quite late Medinan times.

The question of when the *sūras*, or in some cases individual verses or groups of verses, were revealed raises the issue of the relationship of the message to its historical setting. Muslim scholars have always recognized a chronological order of *sūras*, divided into those produced in Muḥammad's Meccan period as Prophet and those revealed in Medina when the *Umma* had been founded and Muḥammad was responsible also for the leadership of a complex political, social, military, and religious order. The Meccan *sūras* are characterized by warnings of a coming divine judgment, when sinners will be punished with hellfire and believers rewarded with heaven. The language is vivid and passionate, with dramatic oaths, bold metaphors, and oracular outbursts. God's "signs" in nature and historical happenings are frequently emphasized as evidences of his providential relationship to the world and humankind. Stories of religious leaders of old, prophets like Abraham, Moses, and Jesus, are cited as antecedents to the Qur'ān and Muḥammad's prophetic activity among the Arabs. The Medinan *sūras* contain many of the same themes as the Meccan ones, but they are also definitively marked by a concern for legal and practical communal matters that reflect the founding and early development of the *Umma* as a total human way of life.

A typical example of a Meccan passage of the Qur'ān is the following, about how the individual will be made to know his or her status on the Last Day:

> When the sun shall be covered up,
> And when the stars swoop down,
> And when the mountains are set moving,
> And when the pregnant camel is abandoned,
> And when the wild beasts are herded together,
> And when the seas are made to overflow,
> And when the souls shall be joined (to their bodies),
> And when the buried-alive infant is asked
>   For what sin she was put to death,
> And when the pages are spread out,
> And when the firmament shall be pulled down,
> And when Hell shall be set blazing,
> And when the Garden is brought near,
> Then shall a soul know what it has produced (81:1–14).

This dramatic passage, from the early Meccan *sūra* called "The Darkening," achieves its impact through symbolic reversals. The sun shines much of the time in Arabia; the stars were traditionally believed to be constant in their courses; the mountains were called by the Old Arabian poets "tent pegs" of the firmament; the pregnant camel was never abandoned in tribal society, because it was the most valuable type of property; and infant girls were sometimes put to death by being buried alive, so as to prevent dishonor to the father and other male relatives if the girl should stray when grown up. Muḥammad and other morally sensitive Arabs of his time considered female infanticide to be the ugliest evidence of a generally decaying social and ethical order in their day. The coming of Judgment Day is to be accompanied by the near approach of blazing hellfire and a cool, shady heaven. All secrets will then be known and all acts weighed for their merit or demerit.

Typical Medinan passages of the Qur'ān, in contrast, read as follows:

> The adulterer and the adulteress, scourge each one of them with a hundred stripes. And do not allow pity for the two to keep you from obeying God, if you believe in God and the Last Day. And let a party of believers witness the punishment. (24:2)

> O believers, Do no enter houses not your own without first announcing your presence and invoking peace on their occupants. (24:27)

> And marry of the spouseless among you, also the upright among your male and female slaves; if they are poor, God will enrich them of His bounty; God is comprehending and aware (24:32)

Note the practical, community-oriented content. The first passage, about people taken in adultery, goes on to prescribe four witnesses to the act. This has remained part of Islamic law, as have many other passages treating specific social and ritual matters.

It would be misleading, however, to cite only Medinan passages that have a practical purpose and subject matter. Some of the most memorable and operative spiritual and ethical passages in the Qur'ān were revealed in the busy, conflict-filled Medinan period of

Muḥammad's prophetic career. One is the "Throne Verse," which is often copied out and worn as an amulet.

> God: there is no god but He, the Living, the Eternal; slumber overtakes Him not, nor sleep. To Him belong whatever is in the heavens and whatsoever is in the earth. Who is there that will intercede with Him except by His permission? He knows that which is in front of them and what is behind them, while they comprehend nothing of His knowledge except what He wills. His throne includes the heavens and the earth, and He is never weary of preserving them. He is the Sublime, the Mighty (2:255).

Another Medinan verse that expresses something of the mysteries of God's nature is the "Light Verse," which Sufi mystics have especially applied to their meditation practices:

> God is the Light of the heavens and the earth. His light is like a niche in which is a lamp, the lamp in a glass and the glass like a brilliant star, lit from a blessed tree, an olive neither of the East nor of the West whose oil would almost give light even though no fire did touch it; light upon light; God guides to His light whomsoever He wills; God coins parables for the people, and God knows everything (24:35).

Our final example of a Medinan verse that transcends the immediate situation of the *Umma* in those days is found in "The Sura of the Cow." Whereas the previous two passages tell about God, this one sets forth what it means to be truly pious as a believing servant of God:

> Truly pious conduct is not turning your faces to the east or to the west; truly good is the one who believes in God and the Last Day and the angels and the Book and the prophets; and gives his wealth, for love of Him, to relatives, and orphans, and the poor, and the one along the way [who suffers because of conversion to Islam], and to set captives free; who observes the *Ṣalat* and pays the *Zakāt*; those who fulfill their covenant when they have entered into one, who endure steadfastly under adversity and hardship, and in time of trouble; these are the ones who have spoken truth, they are the truly devout (2:177).

Muslims preserve and learn and apply their Scripture because of the guidance it contains in the way of information about God and his commands for Muslims individually and collectively. This may be called the "informative" level of Qur'ānic use, because it emphasizes knowledge. But Muslims also preserve and receive spiritual guidance from the Qur'ān through carefully regulated ritual recitation, which ideally must always be done in as beautiful a manner as possible by means of chanting. This level of Qur'ānic use in the community may be called the "performative" level, because it centers in the utterance of and listening to God's sacred words. Surely Muslims strive both to understand the Qur'ān's message even as they enjoy its beautiful recitation as an aesthetic blessing, but the very sounds of Qur'ānic Arabic, when properly chanted, bring people to high planes of spiritual experience and delight. This is experienced even among Muslims who have little or no comprehension of Arabic, at least at the informative level. They may, it is sometimes admitted, "know" the Qur'ān at its deepest, most moving level, even though they do not understand what is literally being said. Most Muslims try to learn the general gist of what they hear of recitation, whether by means of translations or summaries. But ritual performance of the highest caliber does not absolutely imply literal understanding of the text, even by quite skilled reciters who have learned by rote.

The Qur'ān is the central reality of Islamic existence without which the tradition would not have come into being. Scholars have compared the Qur'ān in the Islamic context to Christ in the Christian religion—each is considered to be God's holy Word. In the Christian message the Word is believed to have come down into the world of history as a human being, Jesus of Nazareth. Muslims believe that God sent his Word into the world as a living recitation and a written book, the two being complementary aspects of the central phenomenon of God's presence through sacred speech. Christians partake of the body and blood of Christ symbolically through the sacrament of Communion. Muslims, it may be said, "partake" of the nature of their Lord by means of reciting the Qur'ān. When the Qur'ān is recited properly, God's presence, in the form of his **sakīna**, is believed to descend upon the reciter and hearers. This *sakīna* is a "tranquility," literally, which includes the sense of a protecting and guiding spiritual presence. (Compare this with the Jewish notion of *shekhinah*, "the Presence of God in the world.")

Just as all mindful Muslims know how to perform the *Ṣalāt* and observe the other Pillars of Islam, so do most also know how to recite the Qur'ān, at least at a rudimentary level. Short of that, they know how to respect their holy book and how to listen to its recitation properly. Muslims handle the physical copies of the Qur'ān only in a ritually pure state (because the text itself contains such a command). They honor it by always placing it in a clean and exalted place, never under anything else. And they do not write in the pages of the text, although it is permissible to make notations in a commentary of the Qur'ān.

It is considered to be a specially meritorious achievement to memorize the entire Qur'ān and such a person has been honored as "guardian" of the revelation. The Qur'ān was first revealed orally to Muḥammad, who in turn mastered the text and recited it to his companions. Since that time, the Qur'ān has been transmitted orally as well as in written form down through the generations.

The ritual recitation of the Qur'ān can be performed and appreciated by most Muslims, but its scholarly interpretation is a task

Qur'ān reciters at the shrine of Sunan Ampel, Surabaya, East Java, during the saint's mawlid *or birthday festival. Many other Muslim personages are also buried in the cemetery adjoining the Sunan Ampel mosque.*

reserved for the relatively few who have the intelligence, training, and leisure to master the difficult sciences connected with exegesis: Arabic grammar and rhetoric, the history of the text and its dialectal variants, the principles of interpretation (hermeneutics is the modern term), the history of interpretation, and other matters. Qur'ān interpretation is known in Islam as **tafsīr**, "explanation." There have been different types of *tafsīr*, but the main ones are: literal interpretation, using ancient traditions handed down from the early scholars; rationalistic interpretation, which has a strong theological bias and prefers to treat the Qur'ān as a self-consistent, endlessly revealing spiritual sourcebook not at all limited by traditional views; and allegorical exegesis, preferred usually by mystical types who discern various levels of symbolic meaning in the text, each appropriate to a different plane of spiritual insight and understanding.

The Prophet's Sunna

Muḥammad's success as prophet to the Arabs rested in no small measure on his charismatic personality, which was expressed in wise teaching and balanced judgment on a great variety of matters. Like Moses, he led the people as military commander, preached to them as spiritual counselor, and judged them according to God's law. Muḥammad married and had a large active family. He was constantly in the public eye, yet he also cultivated a thoroughly disciplined private spiritual life of prayer, meditation, fasting, and retreat. In his own life, people came to regard his words as infallible and his acts and gestures as worthy of imitation.

The ancient Arabs called by the term *sunna* any established "way," whether it was a way of living, a procedure, or an actual physical "beaten path" to someplace. *Sunna* contains an implicit imperative, in that it is a recommended way. After Muḥammad died, the Muslims continued to seek guidance from him by remembering his words and acts. These were preserved in verbal reports, or traditions, called *ḥadīths*. If, after consulting the Qur'ān on a matter of importance, nothing could be found to guide individuals or the community on a particular problem or decision, then the recollection of Muḥammad's Sunna was done in hopes of finding a solution. The Muslims who initiated this practice were succeeded by generations of increasingly scholarly collectors and authenticators of *ḥadīths* of the Prophet. There eventually came into being a full-fledged science of *ḥadīth*, which coexisted and served as a kind of complement to the evolving scholarly disciplines connected with interpretation of the Qur'ān as well as with jurisprudence and historical studies.

> Abū Bakr Abī Shaybata and Abū Kurayb reported: they said "Wakī related to us from Mis'ar, [who got it] from Waṣīl, from Abī Wā'īl, from Hudhayfa, that the Messenger of God (May God bless him and give him peace) met him [i.e., a certain companion named Abū Hurayra] and he was sexually polluted, and he turned away from him and performed the major ablution. Then he came and said: 'I was sexually polluted.' And he [i.e., Muḥammad] declared: 'A Muslim is never polluted.' "[5]

This *ḥadīth*, like all such reports, is in two main parts: the first part is the chain of transmitters, which is traced back as completely as possible to an eyewitness of the Prophet's teaching or gesture; the second part is the actual story or report containing the information about what Muḥammad said or did. It is essential that a properly authenticated *ḥadīth* have a sound chain of transmitters, and a special "science of men" was developed to collect and verify biographies of people whose names feature in the transmission of *ḥadīth*

The interesting *ḥadīth* quoted above contains an important detail about the interpretation of ritual impurity. Muḥammad's intent in his sweeping denial of "pollution" attaching to a Muslim was that such a committed person is rightly guided and properly attuned to his *fiṭra*; although sexual intercourse still renders him or her unfit for *Ṣalāt* and other rites, there is no *essential* pollution of the person who is a Muslim. That is, the *person* is not polluted; rather the person is in an impure state, which is transitory. It is not difficult to imagine a rich and detailed discussion arising over this matter, and Muslim legal experts have traditionally been as ingenious and comprehensive as Jewish rabbis in their devotion to and even love of extended debate on legal and religious topics.

A number of reliable collections of *ḥadīth* were achieved by the third Islamic century, with six being especially well regarded. Of those six, two collections, one by al-Bukhārī (d. 870) and another by Muslim ibn al-Ḥajjāj (d. 875), stand out for their high standards, which earned each collection the name "sound." There are many *ḥadīths* common both to Sunnī and Shī'ite Muslims, but there are also separate Shī'ite collections that contain much about the Prophet's family. Many thousands of *ḥadīths* were finally collected by scholars, as many as 600,000 by al-Bukhārī alone. However, a certain percentage of these are the same report, but with differing chains of transmitters. And a large number of *ḥadīths* discovered by such severe judges as al-Bukhārī and Muslim were found to be fraudulent or to suffer from lesser defects. Nevertheless, al-Bukhārī's collection contains about 2,600 different reports and Muslim's a bit over 3,000 (not counting repetitions with differing chains of transmitters).

The *ḥadīth* cover a multitude of subjects and comprise a sort of summation, alongside the Qur'ān, of all that can and should pertain to the Islamic religion and the Muslim way of life. *Ḥadīth* collections contain sections on such topics as God, faith, eschatology, worship (detailed instructions on the Pillars, for example), warfare, marriage and family life, divorce, inheritance, proper deportment and etiquette, food, clothing, toilette (e.g., cutting the nails, growing a moustache, dressing the hair), bodily functions and hygiene, travel, conversation, trade, funerals, Qur'ān recitation and proper procedures for handling the Qur'ān, interpretation of specific Qur'ān verses, details of Muḥammad's life and biographies of his family members and companions, and other things.

Sunna and Umma

A major reason why the Muslim community enjoys such a high degree of uniformity across vast and diverse cultural, geographic, and linguistic boundaries is the Sunna of Muḥammad. The Sunna has provided specific guidance on what a Muslim must believe and do so as to preserve the *Umma*'s distinctiveness, which is a mark of the people of God. There is something soteriological or "saving" about being part of the *Umma*, and the Sunna, passed down from parent to child over the generations, preserves something of the genius and temperament of the Prophet in the hearts and life patterns of the Muslims. Just bearing the name "Muḥammad" is believed by most Muslims to lead toward paradise. The *imitatio Muḥammadi* (comparable to the imitation of Christ in Christianity) has constituted a deep structure in the life of the *Umma* since the rise of Islam. It would be as difficult to imagine Islam without Muḥammad as without the Qur'ān.

It should be apparent that, far from being learned from books, the *ḥadīth* are learned from *living* examples and *living* teaching, by persons who themselves have striven to be at home on the "Muḥammadan" path by internalizing his Sunna. When we consider the crucial importance of the study—in fact the actual memorization—of the Qur'ān and also take into account the Muslims' practice of all the key elements in Muḥammad's Sunna, we realize how the *Shahāda* becomes internalized in a thorough and concrete fashion. We must remember that the Qur'ān and *ḥadīth* do not guide the Muslims primarily as books, that is, as *written* texts; rather, the Muslims themselves become, as it were, "textualized" and activated in such a way as to be in turn a living guide for others. The *Umma* as community of faith is sustained and its peculiar identity secured by the Qur'ān and Sunna as they are incorporated through intimate and indelible processes of personality formation and imprinting and habits of the mind, body, and heart.

Although the Qur'ān is considered by Muslims to be the true words of God and the Sunna to contain the record of Muḥammad's human life and teaching, there is nevertheless a close relationship between the two. Muslims know that the heart of their beloved Prophet can be discerned in every verse of the Qur'ān. They also believe that in the Sunna they have a veritable living commentary on the scriptural revelation.

There is also a third level—beyond Qur'ān and prophetic *ḥadīth*—of sacred guidance for the Muslims in the form of the "Divine Saying" (*ḥadīth qudsī*) couched in Muḥammad's words but purporting to be inspired by God. Divine sayings take as their subject matter spiritual and ethical issues and have thus been especially influential in Muslim piety, particularly of the mystical Sufi sort. Some examples: "My mercy prevails over My wrath." "I was a hidden treasure and desired to be known; therfore I created the creation in order that I might be known." "My Earth and My Heaven contain Me not, but the heart of My faithful servant contains Me." In the Divine Saying we see the closest possible identification between the mind and will of God and the spiritual consciousness of Muḥammad. Indeed, Muḥammad is reported once to have declared:

"He that hath seen me hath seen God." [6] Although this declaration would be considered idolatrous by very strict Muslims, it does reveal something of the Prophet's functional divinity at the popular level.

The *Sharī'a:* God's Legislation for the *Umma*

The solid community structure of the Muslim *Umma* is informed and regulated by the *Sharī'a*, the "way" that has been ordained by God and set forth in the Qur'ān and Sunna. But Scripture and Muḥammad's teaching are not, by themselves, capable of application without a form and method. These have been developed in the various schools of Islamic jurisprudence (**fiqh**) that arose over the first three centuries of Islam. *Sharī'a* as a concept is similar to the Jewish notion of Torah, the "law" or "instructions" governing Jewish teachings and practices. It includes actual law, but transcends law by defining the whole reality of how God relates to humankind in a covenant relationship of Lord and servants. Humans are God's servants but they also are privileged as God's "caliphs" with the charge to manage affairs aright on earth and in historical existence. The *Sharī'a*, then, is a noble idea and firm conviction about the way of the universe, which is in God's hands. The *Sharī'a* is the instrumentality by which the Muslim community persists through the generations in a close bond among its members, which in turn is made possible only by the close bond each Muslim has with God. The rule of the *Sharī'a* among the people of God is the essence or heart of Islam. "Let there be one Umma of you, calling to goodness, and enjoining the right and prohibiting the wrong. Those are the successful ones" (3:104).

Fiqh: Islamic Jurisprudence and Theology

Islamic orthopraxy has always emphasized law over theology, the consequences of actions over the merely theoretical dimensions of intellect. Intellect is essential, but it should be cultivated only in the service of "enjoining the right and prohibiting the wrong." Learning beyond the practical needs of the faith has very often been suspect among Muslims. This suspicion applied largely to intellectual theorizing about God of a purely speculative, academic and ruminative kind. The useful sciences—medicine, astronomy, geography, tactics and strategy, mathematics, chemistry, and so forth—have enjoyed distinguished careers in Islamic civilization, as have also music, literature, and fine arts and philosophy. But systematic theology, in the sense that it is cultivated in Christianity, is decidedly secondary in importance to jurisprudence in Islam and is in fact only a sub-category under it. Known as "the science of discourse," its use has generally been restricted to specialists who have cultivated it for the defense of Islam.

The two greatest sources of jurisprudence in Islam are the Qur'ān and Sunna. Most issues can be treated using a teaching from one or the other or both in consort. And even when it is not possible to find specific guidance in Qur'ān or Sunna, Muslim legal experts have traditionally been able to proceed by means of analogy. In the early generations, when *fiqh* (the term literally means "understanding") was emerging in response to the practical needs of Muslim communities extending over an increasingly large empire, scholars applied the revelation and example of Muḥammad, and indeed of other worthies of his time, along with their own considered personal opinion. Gradually, however, there came into being a limited number of legal schools that were recognized as authoritative, whether by Sunnīs or Shī'ites. Four principal sources of *fiqh* came to be standard for Sunnīs: Qur'ān, Sunna, community consensus, and analogical reasoning. The third source, consensus (**ijmā'**), is followed only by Sunnīs, who have a strong belief in the infallibility of the *Umma*, based on the famous *ḥadīth* attributed to Muḥammad: "Truly, my *Umma* will never agree together on an error." In practice, consensus has prevailed in Sunnī law schools as the most influential of the sources of *fiqh*, because by means of it the Muslims have been able to relate all important matters to what was believed to have been the earliest consensus concerning the Qur'ān, Muḥammad's teachings, and the positions of the pious forebears in the first generations. Consensus is a very conservative force and has often come to block new ways of thinking about and applying both Qur'ān and Sunna to new developments and needs.

The conservatism of Islam has been both a blessing and a bane for the *Umma*. Traditional Muslim scholarship considered that all major questions of belief and law had been aired and settled by around the fourth century after the *Hijra*. Up until then, Muslim jurists, known throughout the *Umma* by the collective term **'ulamā'** ("learned"), had exercised their professional right of independent legal decision making, called **ijtihād**. This technical term derives from the same root as *jihād* and thus carries the meaning of "exertion," too, but in the intellectual sense. An independent Muslim jurist is known as a *mujtahid*. Consensus, at least among Sunnī Muslims, came eventually to regard the "gate" of *ijtihād* as closed. Henceforth, legal scholars and judges would be guided by "imitation" of the ancient and sound worthies in the field of jurisprudence. This imitation eventually proved exceedingly burdensome to alert legal specialists who discerned alternate valid ways of interpreting the Qur'ān and Sunna in matters of law. A number of them, such as the great Damascus legal expert and theologian Ibn Taymīya (d. 1328), continued to claim the right of *ijtihād* and in the process moved Islamic jurisprudence ahead creatively, although they sometimes suffered censure and persecution from the more conservative legists, who usually were in the majority. Since the eighteenth century C.E., more and more Muslims have been calling for reopening of the gate of *ijtihād* so as to update and extend in rationally sound ways the *Sharī'a* in the modern world, which has presented unforeseen and complex challenges to the *Umma*.

Shī'ites and Sunnīs

Shī'ite Muslims have never ceased exercising *ijtihād*. They have persisted in their different subcommunities in maintaining an honored place for independent legal reasoning, in the belief that God guides them through the divine light descending from Muḥammad through 'Alī and several Imāms or divinely guided "leaders" of Shī'ism. Shī'ite *fiqh*, consequently, has been considerably more flexible and adaptive than Sunnī jurisprudence, although there are also certain areas where the two inevitably and willingly overlap and mutually reinforce each other; that is, Sunnīs and Shī'ites are equally Muslim, and the two divisions of the Umma, even though the former numbers around 80 percent, do consider each other to be members of the same tradition of faith, order, and community. Their sometimes pronounced (and tragic) differences over rule and political theory as well as other matters nevertheless did not result in anything as drastic as the theological, liturgical, legal, and denominational divisions that Christianity experienced. Thus, although such comparisons are perilous, Shī'ites and Sunnīs are closer to each other in liturgical, legal, and even theological essentials than Christian groups such as Episcopalians and Baptists. In the liturgical dimension—which includes the Pillars, and especially the *Ṣalāt* and the *Ḥajj*—Shī'ites and Sunnīs are virtually identical.

Sunnī Islam has dominated in most periods and places, at least politically. The great 'Abbāsid dynasty (750–1258C.E.), although it was launched with the help and ideas of Shī'ism, soon revealed its Sunnī basis and suppressed Shī'ite movements during its long history. But in Iraq, and later even more in Iran, Shī'ism, continued to maintain loyal followings. By the fifteenth and sixteenth centuries, Iran came increasingly to be dominated by Shī'ite principles and figures, thus establishing its character down to the present, when Shī'ite religious scholars and judges are in complete control of the revolutionary Islamic regime under the leadership of the Ayatollah ("Sign of God") Khomeini; Khomeini rules as a *mujtahid* and as the sole contemporary representative of the last divinely guided *Imām*, who disappeared in the early Islamic centuries and is believed to be preserved by God in an occult state of concealment until the time comes for him to return in judgment at the end of time.

Although the *Sharī'a*, theoretically, rules all of Muslim life, in the present only a few countries are earnestly applying it—Saudi Arabia, Iran, and Pakistan are the most noteworthy. It is difficult to govern by the medieval *Sharī'a* in the complex world of today, when all countries depend to some extent on an international economic, political, and military order, with the great powers forcing alliances, if only by default, and a host of peoples and societies not governed by Islamic principles impinging on the *Umma* in countless ways. Aspects of these problems, especially when faced by Muslims in the contemporary West, will be considered in the last chapter.

The *Ṭarīqa:* Personal Piety and the Quest for Union with God

As crucially important and pervasive as Muslim regard for the *Sharī'a* and its right ordering of life in service to God is, to the extent that Islam fully deserves the characterization of "orthoprax" that we have given it throughout this book, Muslims also know another major way of being religious. This way is known as the **Ṭarīqa**, an Arabic word that, like *Sharī'a*, also means "way," but includes the sense of a spiritual discipline or path, rather than God's legislation in the external sense of law and correct procedures for the *Umma* as a whole. The *Ṭarīqa* is the interior way of mystically inclined Muslims. Unlike the *Sharī'a*, it is not in any sense official or required to be maintained and applied. Rather, Muslims follow the *Ṭarīqa* because of inward urgings and personal questings for a more intimate religious life of closeness to God and to like-minded spiritual seekers.

Because of the interior aspect of the *Ṭarīqa*, its forms of expression and institutionalization have been many and varied. The name that is given to these forms of personal spirituality is "Sufism," a term with a fascinating history. In early Islamic times, after Muslims had succeeded in conquering and coming to dominate many regions of the Middle East and North Africa, there came into being a kind of spiritual reaction to the wealth and ease that people were enjoying in various centers of the *Umma*. The formal ritual observances of *Ṣalāt, Zakāt*, fasting in Ramaḍān, the *Ḥajj,* and related acts continued to be the center of orthoprax Islam, to be sure, but increasing numbers of Muslims wanted also a more familiar and informal dimension to their religious lives. And a good number also considered the wealth and pleasures of this world to be a trap, tempting them to lose sight of their obligations and the life of the world to come. There were some who took to wearing patched woolen frocks as a sign of renunciation of the world and reliance on God's grace alone. Before long, this woolen garment gave to the new fashion of ascetic piety the name of *ṣūfī*, from the Arabic word *ṣūf*, "wool."

The Muslim mystics came to express their religious convictions in many new ways and with distinctive forms of ritual and communal etiquette. Sufism did not, except for some extremist exponents, depart from the universal religious duties of Muslims; rather it may be understood to have intensified them and augmented them with new rites and ceremonies. These last centered in remembering God by mentioning in prayerlike formulas his "Most Beautiful Names," as the Qur'ān calls them, which are believed to number ninety-nine. The "mentioning" of God often is commanded of all Muslims by the Qur'ān, but the Sufis came to focus on this practice more than all others. This practice of mentioning is known as **dhikr** and it took on a variety of forms, from plain voiced repetition of Qur'ānic words and phrases in a rhythmic manner, to silent forms of inner meditation with elaborate breathing exercises, to enraptured dance to the music of flutes and drums until the performers fell down in swoons of ecstasy in union with their Lord.

From its beginnings, Sufism emphasized the place of the spiritual master, or **shaykh**, who was always believed to have received esoteric doctrine through a line of spiritual guides traceable back to the Prophet Muḥammad, whom all Muslims consider to be the perfect human master, imbued with God's blessing and wisdom. Although many different doctrines and practices developed in an unregulated and translegal environment of *Ṭarīqa* cultivation, there was the governing conviction among Sufis that God through the Qur'ān and Muḥammad through his Sunna were the ultimate authorities and sustaining power of their diverse institutional modes of doctrine and meditation. The charter event of the *Ṭarīqa* and of all the individual orders that embodied it in most parts of the Muslim world was the mysterious Night Journey and Ascension of Muḥammad from Mecca to Jerusalem and up through the seven heavens to the presence of God. This meeting of Muḥammad with his Lord provides unlimited inspiration to Sufis, as well as other Muslims, who see it as the completion of the relationship between God and his Prophet: first God sent down his Word in the form of the Qur'ān, then he lifted his servant Muḥammad up to his own abode. God condescended to earth so that his faithful creature could ascend to heaven. Just as Jesus' life, passion, and resurrection are seen by Christians to be moments in a great redemptive epic, whereby all those baptized in Christ believe that they will inherit eternal life with him and the Father in heaven, so also do Muslims consider Muḥammad's Ascension to be crucial proof of God's promise of success in a blessed afterlife with him. Muḥammad was raised up to heaven in this life, and the Sufis especially have deduced important religious principles from Muḥammad's Ascension.

The main deduction of Sufism with regard to Muḥammad's Ascension is that others, too, may experience God directly and definitively in this life. The aim of Sufi meditation, then, came to be the gradual purifying of the lower self of all things pertaining to this world, until the higher self could experience annihilation and unification with God. Once the Sufi experiences loss of his or her own ego, then God takes over indeed and transforms the person into a being intimately entwined with himself. The precise way in which this is believed to occur inspired various theories and forms of expression, all of which admittedly are imperfect as such, but nevertheless attempt to characterize in words what is finally beyond human ability to verbalize. The experience, the actual "tasting" of union with God, is the important thing, whether or not mere human intellect can grasp it.

Sufism took on institutional form as doctrines and schools first and later as actual organizations, "brotherhoods" which came to spread from country to country. The earliest Sufis, like the great theologian and legal scholar Ḥasan of Baṣra (d. 728), tended toward asceticism and a very sober and often sad view of life, which included weeping for one's sins and despairing of salvation. Although an ascetic mode has continued to inspire and inform Sufis down to the present, before long it was more love than sorrow that came to characterize the *Ṭarīqa*. A remarkable woman saint, Rābi'a al-'Adawīya (d. 801), discovered in her solitary vigils with God, often lasting all night, that love was at the core of the universe; not to reflect and relate this love to those around us and back to God was to renounce our highest privilege. Rābi'a's conviction that the love in the believer's heart is itself a response to God's prior love was expressed memorably by a later saint, Jalāl al-Dīn Rūmī (d. 1273), whose thousands of Persian rhymed couplets contain the entire spectrum of Sufi emotion and reflection.

> Never, in sooth, does the lover seek without being sought by his beloved.
> When the lightning of love has shot into *this* heart, know that there is love in *that* heart.
> When love of God waxes in thy heart, beyond any doubt God hath love of thee.
> The soul says to her base earthly parts, "My exile is more bitter than yours: I am celestial."
> The body desires green herbs and running water, because its origin is from those;
> The soul desires Life and the Living One, because its origin is the Infinite Soul.
> The desire of the soul is for ascent and sublimity; the desire of the

> body is for self and means of self-indulgence
> And that Sublimity desires and loves the soul: mark the text *He loves them and they love Him.*[7] (emphasis mine)

This last line is the favorite passage in the Qur'ān for Sufis—5: 59.

There have been different kinds of Sufis as well as Sufi organizations and meditation paths. Sufis have sometimes divided themselves into three types: "sober," "antinomian," and "intoxicated." The first type of Sufis are really normal pious Muslims, but they have a capacity to experience the depths of what the *Sharī'a* prescribes by way of ritual worship practices. In fact, every Muslim should be a Sufi in this sense. And very many are, without using the title "Sufi," because of the strong conviction that God's friends, those whom he loves, are all who submit to him and love him, too. Muḥammad and his companions, as well as members of the Prophet's family, are considered to be the soberest of Sufis, if Sufis they are considered to be at all, for they lived before the term"Sufism" was coined.

The antinomian type of Sufi is a type of religious person known in other traditions, marked by resistance to moral and ritual rules as hampering spiritual spontaneity. He or she may go to extremes, like even violating certain commands of the *Sharī'a*, e.g., refusing to perform the *Ṣalāt*; or one of these types might simply not exhibit any obvious piety, for fear of being praised and thus placed in danger of prideful self-esteem and thus, eventually, damnation. The antinomian Sufis wanted to bring blame upon themselves, following a Qur'ānic passage (12:53) that has been interpreted to mean that it is required for true believers to blame their own carnal selves so as to prepare the higher self for union with God. Various opinions, from highly laudatory to vituperative, have been held about the antinomian Sufis, but the type persists.

The third type are the intoxicated Sufis who delight in the ecstatic transport they experience in close union with God. These "drunken" Sufis did not gain their reputation by drinking actual alcoholic beverages (intoxicants are forbidden in Islam); rather, they expressed their brimming joy mostly by means of beautiful poetry, often centering on the theme of wine and taverns of a heavenly character. This wine is God's love, which inspires, intoxicates and transforms the true seeker, just as in paradise there will be a delightful drink that thrills like earthly wine but has no negative effect or hangover.

Sufism makes for a fascinating and rewarding study, but to go further into the subject here would require considerable additional historical, doctrinal, and literary discussion. Suffice it to say that Sufism has often been called the "heartbeat" of Islam, in that it provides the inner dynamic and delight of being a Muslim, whereas the *Sharīʻa* provides the external regulating structure for Muslims in community. Working together, the *Sharīʻa* as the exoteric and the *Ṭarīqa* as the esoteric dimensions of Islam, the *Umma* enjoys a balanced and inspirited life. The *Sharīʻa* enables the *Umma* to proceed securely through history by regulating matters of common faith and order, while the *Ṭarīqa* convinces its followers that God is very near, indeed, and in close communion with his special "friends" (*walīs*), as the Sufis like to characterize themselves. As the Qur'ān declares: "Surely God's friends—no fear shall be on them, neither shall they sorrow" (10:63). The American poet of the last century Emily Dickinson wrote a short poem about keeping the Sabbath. Some keep it going to church, while others stay at home "with a bobolink for a chorister and an orchard for a dome." Dickinson, who stayed at home, ended her poem by declaring that while those who strive at religion through church services "get to heaven at last, I'm going all along." The Sufis are not content to wait for heaven at last, either; they want it now.

This chapter has described the main structures of Islamic belief and practice, within the context of the strong community that is the *Umma*. In the next chapter, we shall consider some of the dynamics of Muslim faith and order by describing and analysing representative institutions in greater detail.

CHAPTER IV:

Representative Muslim Institutions and Their Dynamics

The knowledge of Islam's structures of faith and practice, Scripture and tradition, law and spirituality is in itself insufficient for gaining a rounded appreciation of the quality of Muslim life. The Qur'ān is of central importance for all dimensions of Islamic belief and life, and we know that its appropriation by the believers is both intellectual—aimed at understanding the message's meaning—and practical—devoted to spiritual power and guidance by means of ritual recitation. But the actual human institutions by which the Qur'ān is mastered also need to be described. The description provided in this chapter on dynamics will aid in understanding some of the ways in which the Qur'ān is received, enjoyed and applied among Muslims. Our focus will be on recitation.

The second major dimension of Muslim life to be treated in this chapter is somewhat different from the appropriation of the Qur'ān. Qur'ān-based education is universal and provides most of the formal matter by which Islam is authenticated as true, but there is another way in which Muslims in many but not all regions cultivate their religious lives beyond the study of their sacred book. Muslims also recognize the importance of sacred *persons* whom they venerate and from whom they seek guidance, boons, and intercession with God. They do this principally by means of specific cults that have grown up around the burial places of holy persons, "saints." Even with the immeasurably great guides of Qur'ān and Sunna to regulate and inspire them, Muslims prove by their beliefs and practices related to the veneration of saints that it is impossible for most people to be generic Muslims, that is, detached from specific, local, often folk cultures that antedate, coexist with, and sometimes even compete with scriptural, "official" Islam.

The third and final dimension to be examined in this chapter is the Muslim lifecycle, the stages of life from birth to death that mark each person's progress in the Muslim way. Like Qur'ānic education, it is universal. And like the practice of the veneration of saints, it also has many local variants and associations. However, unlike saint veneration, it is part of orthoprax Islam in that it is considered by all to be required.

Recitation of the Qur'ān

Qur'ānic Education in Indonesia

As we learned earlier, the recitation of the Qur'ān with at least a minimum level of proficiency is done in all Muslim locales. Initially, native Arabic speakers have an obvious advantage, because although Qur'ānic Arabic is archaic and highly idiomatic compared with modern colloquial dialects of Arabic, it is nevertheless the same language, with many points of convergence and identity with modern spoken and written Arabic. And Arabic-speaking nations have many radio and television programs featuring classical and Qur'ānic Arabic recitations, Friday sermons, theological lectures, and religious discussions.

But Muslims living in non-Arabic-speaking countries also strive to master Arabic well enough for worship and meditation, including reading and recitation of the Qur'ān. In Indonesia, where the Malay-based national language, Bahasa Indonesia, has no linguistic connection with Semitic languages, Indonesian nonetheless contains around two thousand words derived from Arabic, especially in the religious fields. Nearly all the terminology of ritual and religious concepts is based on Arabic words, mostly from the Qur'ān and the Ḥadīth. Since the coming of Islam to the Indonesian arhipelago, beginning in the twelfth and thirteenth centuries and increasing to major proportions by the fifteenth and sixteenth centuries, converts have worked hard to learn Arabic. At first, in Java, for example, recitation of the Qur'ān seems to have been performed in Javanese, using traditional themes and symbols to communicate the story of Islam to a population steeped in aboriginal Javanese as well as imported Hindu and Buddhist lore antedating the coming of Islam.

Centuries ago, Muslim teachers (traditionally male) began establishing small schools on Java and Sumatra. Such a religious teacher in Indonesia is called a **kiai**, which is roughly equivalent to the Arabic *shaykh*, "master." The center of the *kiai's* teaching has traditionally been the text of the Qur'ān, both read and recited. In addition, to the extent that the *kiai* was able to master the materials himself, Ḥadīth materials and other religious texts were included in the curriculum. The Islamic school came to be known as a *pesantren*, the place where *santri*, "orthoprax," Muslim students learn. Thus the institutions of *kiai* and *pesantren* formed the ongoing educational nucleus of Indonesian *santri* Muslim society, introduced in the opening chapter. *Pesantrens* have always been mainly local affairs, to which students go during certain hours of the day or evening for instruction, prayers, and fellowship with other young folk, boys with

"Pondok Modern," in Gontor, near Ponorogo, East Java, Indonesia. This famous pondok pesantren *for boys and young men emphasizes modern subjects, but maintains a strong commitment to Islamic learning and values in its communal life and cooperative self-government. Students and faculty together built the mosque and minaret at the center of the campus, shown here. Many of Indonesia's most important Islamic leaders of recent times were educated here.*

boys and girls with girls. But there are also many residential *pesantrens*, especially in traditionally minded East Java, where students ranging from eight to eighteen years of age or older comprise a cohesive community. A residential *pesantren* is called a **pondok pesantren**, from the Arabic word *funduq*, "hostel," "inn."

Pondok pesantrens today continue to make the Qur'ān and Arabic education the center of the curriculum, but in some cases additional subjects like math, social studies, science, history, and practical arts are also included. Instruction in the Qur'ān and Arabic begins as early as feasible, with students writing on slates or paper tablets, pronouncing the letters, then groups of letters, and short Qur'ānic phrases. Recent years have seen the introduction of a wide range of instruction manuals covering principles of recitation and related matters of etiquette and doctrine. Regional and national Qur'ānic education societies cooperating with Indonesia's Department of Religious Affairs have also developed graded curricular materials for Qur'ānic instruction. Such textbooks are used in *pesantrens* and other, more modern types of schools.

Although the Qur'ān is the backbone of traditional *pondok pesantren* education, the close community of students and *kiai* and other instructors serves as a human laboratory for the socializing of Indonesian youth in habits and patterns of cooperation and consensus that are considered essential to Indonesian personal and communal identity. Indonesians have a strong sense of loyalty to the society as a whole and prefer to subordinate their individual wills and ambitions and blend them into the collective whole of shared values and mutually beneficial disciplines. The close fit between traditional Indonesian social customs and convictions and Islamic doctrines and communal values is fortuitous for both and a major factor in Islam's phenomenal success in being embraced by 90 percent of Indonesians.

Indonesian Muslims, especially the *santri* types who cultivate Qur'ānic literacy and pure *Sharī'a*-based devotional practices and social relations enjoy a combination of close social and cultural identification with their local group and with Javanese, Acehnese, Maduran, or some other ethnic subcommunity along with a transcending Muslim identity, which extends to the whole nation and to all parts of the Muslim world. The ability to read the Qur'ān carries with it the ability to read widely also in the classics of Islamic legal, theological, historical, and devotional literatures. But although most Indonesian Muslims do not possess sufficient Arabic literacy to delve into such classical sources, the minimal Qur'ānic Arabic comprehension they do have permits them to experience a deeply satisfying ritual incorporation into certain patterns and processes of Muslim awareness and intimacy with God and fellow believers that enliven and sustain Muslims everywhere.

Although the *kiai* provides the fundamental instruction for the *pesantren*, he in fact is as often an imposing, serene eminence as he is a constantly or overtly active leader. That is, his leadership consists in large part in setting an example of a wise, virtuous, and commanding personality. He actively teaches, but much of the time the older students work with the younger ones, passing on their superior knowledge and ability, especially in Qur'ānic recitation. Beyond the formal instruction, which may take only a few hours of each day, the students occupy themselves with such household and personal chores as cleaning the premises, tending vegetable gardens, washing clothes, and preparing meals. The *kiai* certainly maintains order and decorum within the *pesantren*; but he also acts as counselor and inspiration to the wider community outside the walls of the *pondok*. Sometimes a *kiai's* fame spreads far, even outside of Indonesia, resulting in parents sending their children to be enrolled for their whole period of adolescent coming of age as Muslims and proper citizens.

In general, the more traditional the *pesantren*, the better the mastery of Qur'ān recitation and Arabic literacy. In some establishments, this includes also the memorization of the Qur'ān, a demanding task that takes a candidate with suitable aptitude and disciplined study habits about three years to achieve. One of the most important factors in memorizing the Qur'ān is a supportive, similarly dedicated community of fellow reciters. And once the Qur'ān has been memorized, it must be kept in memory through continuous review and practice. As the Prophet Muḥammad is reported to have said, "Keep refreshing your knowledge of the Qur'ān, for I swear by Him in whose hands my soul is that it is more liable to escape than camels which are tethered."

A typical *pondok pesantren* has both individual and group Qur'ān recitation as a daily activity. The youngest students are typically taught by older students, beginning with rudimentary instruc-

Advanced student reciting the Qur'ān at the Institute of Qur'ānic Studies, Singosari, East Java, Indonesia. The students concentrate on Qur'ānic education at the residential pondok pesantren, *but attend public school for modern subjects.*

tion in the writing of individual Arabic letters and practicing their sounds. Little groups can be heard pronouncing series of letters, until, when the pronunciation is satisfactory, they are assigned Qur'ānic words, and then whole phrases to recite. The teacher intones the passage and then the students repeat after him, back and forth, sometimes for long periods. The teacher will often mark time, either with hand clapping or by rapping a stick on the desk (the stick is also used for occasional disciplinary measures).

Instruction in recitation in Indonesia is essentially a mimicking process, whereby the teacher's tones and inflections become replicated in the recitation of the students. When the time for recitation of longer Qur'ānic passages comes, an introduction to the quasi-musical elements of true chanting is begun. Such performance is beautiful to the ear and individuals who come to excel in it achieve a special status in each school. In one respected *pesantren* in East Java, the "head boy," who is around twenty, is entrusted with teaching recitation to a large gathering of adults, more than three hundred, who come for a weekly training session. It is impressive to hear the assembly, which is divided by sex into separate but adjoining groups, practicing in unison the ancient Qur'ānic words and phrases as made fresh and vibrant by the mellifluous baritone voice of the preceptor. The *kiai* presides and gives formal instruction, but his student assistant provides the crucially important vocal demonstration and model phrases according to their proper melodies and rhythms. The teaching of eager and grateful townspeople is an example of this particular *pesantren's* Islamic outreach to ordinary folk. The joyful receiving of recitation training by the people is evident in the expressions on their faces and the respectful manner in which they greet and say good-bye to the *kiai* and his assistant. The unison chanting, even of practice phrases, is a thrilling expression of heartfelt praise of God by a class that also considers itself to be a congregation.

One way by which modern Indonesian Qur'ān students maintain high standards of recitation and enjoy the process as well is through contests. In the past twenty years or so the authorities have sponsored local, regional, provincial, and national Qur'ān chanting competitions that cycle over a period of two years, normally, and end in the recognition of individual male and female reciters as the best in the country in youth, adult, and handicapped categories. Awards are made for high achievement in artistic chanting, in memorization of the Qur'ān, and in knowledge about the Qur'ān and its proper uses in piety and the religious sciences.

Wherever the national Qur'ān reciting tournament is held, the host city takes special pride in preparing itself for the many contestants and visitors who spend upwards of two weeks participating in and attending daily and nightly sessions and enjoying Islamic fashion shows, book and cultural exhibits, and other special events. The process preserves high-caliber Qur'ānic competency among succeeding generations of Muslim students, and also unites Indonesian Muslims in the common cause of Islamic mission and revival, both among the believers and in outreach to others.

A national Qur'ān chanting tournament was held in 1985 in Pontianak, the capital of the Indonesian province of West Kalimantan, on the island of Borneo. Before the opening ceremonies there was a parade of around a hundred colorful floats through the city streets; teams from all over the country and local organizations and clubs were represented. The floats were decorated with Qur'ānic calligraphy. The formal opening ceremonies were presided over by President Suharto and officials from the Ministry of Religion and Islamic organizations. A large sports stadium had been transformed into a recitation arena by the erection of a special pulpit of recitation in the center of the playing field.

The opening ceremonies included recitation by the previous winners in the male and female categories, who reigned over the events as a kind of king and queen, complete with crowns. Then, after speeches from dignitaries, the official tournament flag was presented by the president of Indonesia to a special Islamic drill team, which then raised it at the end of the field, next to the flag of the Republic of Indonesia. A large brass band marched briskly around the track leading the twenty-seven provincial recitation teams, each in its regional dress, as they passed in review before the president and gathered officials. After these formalities were over, the second half of the program was introduced, featuring a dance performance by eleven hundred brightly costumed men and women, who spilled out onto the playing field and went through a number of intricate formations including prayer postures, and closing with the spelling out of the logo of the tournament, like an American football band's halftime show. Music was provided by a five-hundred piece orchestra and a mixed Chinese Catholic choir of several thousand voices. Pontianak, which has a non-Muslim, mostly Chinese, ethnic majority, extended its warmest hospitality to the visiting Muslims and joined in the spirit of the chanting tournament, which in Indonesia is viewed as a "national discipline" as well as Islamic piety. The Indonesian national Qur'ān chanting tournament is covered extensively on the national media, with a daily televised recap of events in the evening as part of the national and world news.

Qur'ān recitation competitions are held in other Muslim countries, too, notably Egypt, Saudi Arabia, Brunei, and Malaysia. This last country sponsors the prestigious international Qur'ān reciting contest, which attracts the best reciters from all over the Muslim world. Very often non-native-Arabic-speaking reciters win top honors. Such persons typically have received the kind of intensive exposure to the Qur'ān and specialized training in its recitation that the Indonesian *pondok pesantren* system provides.

Qur'ānic education is available to Indonesians outside *pondok pesantrens*, too, in neighborhood mosques, after-school institutes, and through tutors. Recitation instruction is also available through tape cassettes and accompanying workbooks. Both radio and television carry recitation frequently, and it is common for the final moments of the broadcast day to be devoted to the recitation of Qur'ānic passages before sign-off.

In the large East Java port city of Surabaya, I was present in a studio audience in the provincial television station where a regional Qur'ān recitation competition was held. Each contestant knelt on a raised platform; the open Qur'ān was mounted on a stand in front of him or her. Three lights—green, amber, and red—marked the time in which the performance had to occur; red meant stop, the end of the recitation. The same procedure marks the national tournament. In between groups of reciters, special entertainment was provided by a Muslim rock band of young men and women from the nearby Islamic teachers' college. Performers played guitars, drums, and other instruments and singers swayed back and forth with fingers snapping and eyes flashing in a wholesome display of youthful exuberance. Both sexes were properly dressed; the women wore glitzy ensembles that nevertheless covered both hair and body without concealing a brimming enjoyment of being young and "with it." As I watched, I was led to compare the show with American parallels of rock gospel groups and squeaky-clean evangelistic pop music. Not all Muslim leaders would approve of combining Qur'ān recitation with popular entertainment, whether on the same program or in the same stratum of society, but their integration in a common Muslim youth culture in Surabaya seems not to be too controversial.

It is not uncommon for persons of means in Indonesia to endow an institute for Qur'ānic instruction. I once met a medical school professor from North Sumatra who established such a school for very small children, complete with a special building and a full-time teacher. I asked my friend why he went to such lengths when there were already mosques, *pondok pesantrens*, and other opportunities for learning the Qur'ānic message and the skills of recitation. He replied that he himself had been greatly blessed in his life by the Qur'ān, not only with professional success—which he had surely achieved—but also with the satisfaction of becoming a very accomplished Qur'ān reciter himself. This physician had developed his own approach to recitation training, with which he had had great success with university students in the large city of Medan. His institute for young children was his way of promoting his successful method, which was designed especially for people whose native language is not Arabic. When I was about to say good-bye to my friend and fly across the Malacca Straits to Malaysia, a difficulty was discovered concerning my ticket and my credentials. The doctor inquired and, with a combination of humble patience and savoir-faire, succeeded in smoothing out the difficulty. When I thanked him profusely, he said not to think that *he* had done anything; rather, as he put it, I had experienced "something of the blessings of the Qur'ān." His meaning seemed to be that anyone pursuing knowledge of the Qur'ān—even a Western anthropological fieldworker—could not fail to be rewarded by God in his search.

Scriptural Piety

The contemporary Islamic revival has brought Muslims back to their spiritual roots in the Qur'ān and Sunna. In Cairo, Egypt, for example, one can find Qur'ān recitation training going on in groups of people of very diverse backgrounds and occupations. Recitation teachers, some old and venerable, make the rounds of mosques and homes to provide individual and group instruction. One class that I came to know over the course of several months included a middle-aged computer programmer, a retired banker, a young woman student of religion, and a janitor. Another was made up of a retired government official from the department of textiles, a young professor of veterinary science, a stockbroker, a retired military officer, a teacher of religion, a laborer or two, and others. One of the attractions of the classes, both of which were taught by the same highly revered elderly recitation master, was the privilege of being in frequent contact with him, thereby receiving blessings. Another was the satisfaction of trying to improve one's spiritual life by means of the considerable application that Qur'ānic recitation requires. One person confided that he had not been brought up with religious training and now that he was middle-aged and beginning to ponder his own mortality he thought that the Qur'ān would provide a badly needed sense of security and purpose.

There are a number of technical Arabic terms connected with Qur'ān recitation. One, often used as an overall term for the oral performance aspects of recitation, is **tilāwa**. This term also means "reading" and the root includes in addition the sense of "to follow." I was told by the recitation master mentioned above that *tilāwa* is the most meaningful term for recitation, because it includes the essential element of "following," in the sense of *obeying*, God's message. Without such faithful commitment, beautiful sounding recitation is devoid of spiritual benefits; it is simply musical entertainment.

The Qur'ān has been the main ingredient in providing Muslims security and purpose in all times and places. Although its scientific interpretation and application in ritual and social-legal contexts is a matter for specialists, the Qur'ān overflows the banks of professional boundaries into all areas of personal and communal Muslim life, from popular religious television programs in Indonesia to gatherings of pious folk in Egypt bent on revitalizing and preserving their spiritual and moral lives. The dynamics of Qur'ānic religion are the lifeblood of Islam without which the tradition would eventually vanish. It is significant that, although Muslim theological and legal schools have often been rigid and unable to adapt to changed situations, the Qur'ān and its related piety structures, above all recitation, have continued to motivate, challenge, comfort, and sustain Muslims through the multitude of trials and temptations that their successes as well as their calamities have brought them down through the generations.

The Qur'ānically grounded Muslim—and that is the only true Muslim—is grateful to God for whatever he ordains, serene in the conviction that the steadfast patience he or she is able to muster is itself a sign of God's guidance. To "seek the Face of God," as the Qur'ān characterizes the ultimate quest of Islam, requires approaching him first and last by his word. Reading the Qur'ān in Arabic is a special experience unmatched by any other for Muslims. The power of its sounds and cadences, coupled with its striking expressions, grips readers and hearers and often renders them helpless to resist its sacred "magic." The Qur'ān itself contains many statements and examples of religious experience. The performative aspect of Qur'ānic recitation, introduced earlier, is securely rooted in the text itself. That is, the Qur'ān *does things* to people beyond merely providing an informational message. What it does to readers and hearers through the medium of oral performance is itself a main part of the message. The Qur'ān is like a living, breathing reality, fully aware of itself and its power to inspire.

> The skins of those who fear their Lord shiver from (hearing) it, then their skins and hearts soften at the remembrance of God (39:23).

There comes a moment in the reading of the Qur'ān, as for example in personal study focused on understanding the meaning, whether reciting out loud or reading silently, when readers start feeling an uncanny, sometimes frightening presence. Instead of reading the Qur'ān, the reader begins feeling the Qur'ān is "reading" the reader! This is a wonderfully disturbing experience, by no means requiring a person to be a Muslim before it can be felt. This expression of the Qur'ān's inherent power has been a major factor in the spread of Islam, as well as Muslims' continuing loyalty to the Straight Path, as the Qur'ān itself characterizes the religion.

Islamic legal and theological schools have risen, prospered for a time, then vanished. In today's complex and cosmopolitan world, certain traditional aspects and institutions of Islam, such as rule in accordance with the *Sharī'a*, have been called into question by Muslims and even set aside. But throughout all the change and ferment of modern times, the Qur'ān has continued to provide the central source of meaning, values, and spiritual power for Muslims everywhere. It is one thing for Muslims to study the Qur'ān's literal message and apply it to life. But when difference of opinion and confusion reign and when Muslims find it difficult if not impossible to agree on interpretations and applications of the Qur'ān in actual situations, then the pious recitation of it can still serve as a uniting and empowering force. A colleague once told me about a gathering of Muslim religious experts traveling together on a long bus trip. A violent theological argument broke out, one no one could stop until someone started reciting the Qur'ān. Gradually, the others realized that they were shouting and bickering in the presence of God's manifest speaking. Silence returned and the men repented in the renewed fellowship of receiving God's "tranquility," that *sakīna* which descends when the Word is recited.

Muslim "Saints" and Their Veneration in Popular Islam

Christians have always placed great emphasis on the sanctity of persons. This practice is rooted in the Bible itself. The greatest of all

Christian saints is, of course, Jesus, in whom Christians believe that God himself was pleased to have come into human historical life for the redemption of the race from sin and death. But Jesus is really more than a saint; for Christians, he is the incarnation of God. The church developed an elaborate doctrinal and institutional structure for the recognition and, it could be said, the regulation of sainthood. There even developed a theory that the saints, through their abundant spiritual virtues, provide a treasury of merit that can be dispensed by the pope to penitent sinners who purchase indulgences. The selling of indulgences became one of the main controversies leading to the Lutheran Reformation in the sixteenth century, but the theory of saintly merit and its availability for the remission of punishment in purgatory still stands in Roman Catholicism.

A saint, at least in Christian understanding, is a holy person who is exemplary in conduct and able to perform miracles, or a martyr, or the center of cultic veneration, or all of these. Usually it takes a considerable time after the death of a candidate for sainthood before the official ecclesiastical machinery of canonization produces a certified saint. This has been true especially since around 1000 C.E. Next to Jesus, the Blessed Virgin Mary has been the leading saint of the church.

The Qur'ān, unlike the Bible, never speaks of the holiness of persons, so, strictly speaking, it does not recognize "saints." The word "saint" derives from the Latin *sanctus*, "holy." According to the Qur'ān, God alone is holy, and even there the concept of holiness is not often encountered. The Qur'ānic term rendered in English as saint is *walī*, which actually should be translated "friend." We were introduced to this term at the end of the preceding chapter, in connection with Sufism, which has always placed emphasis on the warm, intimate relationship between God and his human friends.

But, Qur'ānically based arguments notwithstanding, Muslims have in fact considered certain persons to be specially endowed with spiritual power and blessings, which they believe can be bestowed on others. Such potent *walīs* may indeed be recognized for their sanctity during their lifetimes, but most often it is after their deaths that a cult grows around their memory and their mortal remains, represented in burial shrines humble and grand found in most Muslim regions.

In Egypt, for example, the cult of Muslim saints exists alongside the veneration of Christian saints, and the two sometimes overlap and mingle at certain seasons and in special places. There is a cultural dimension in Egypt that exhibits great sensitivity toward persons and objects believed to contain spiritual power, known in Arabic as **baraka**. Both Upper and Lower Egypt have had distinct cultural identities since prehistoric times. But both regions, the long, narrow Nile Valley extending upstream from Cairo toward the lakes of Central Africa and the lowlands of the Delta, where the branches of the Nile meander until they reach their Mediterranean mouths at Damietta and Rosetta, enjoy exuberant growths of saint cults in hamlets, towns, and cities everywhere.

There is something in traditional Egyptian attitudes that considers a human habitation without a resident saint as somehow lacking an essential element for full life. As noted earlier, returning Egyptian pilgrims who have made the Meccan *Ḥajj* often have the outside walls of their houses painted with *Ḥajj* scenes and sacred texts. A *Ḥājjī* is a kind of living saintly presence in an Egyptian village. But most Egyptian saints, whether Christian or Muslim, are spiritual beings who have lived on after their biological deaths. In some cases, appropriate burial edifices have been erected to their memories because of uncanny post-death events such as visitations to the living in dreams and visions. Not all such saints are pleasant or beneficial; sometimes they are threatening and disposed to carrying out destructive acts if suitable recognition of their cultic demands is not forthcoming.

The greatest Egyptian Muslim saint is **Sayyid** (a title borne by descendants of Muḥammad) Aḥmad al-Badawī, a thirteenth-century Sufi master originally from Morocco, who settled in the Delta city of Tanta and built a large, loyal following there. He is remembered principally through major celebrations held several times a year at the mosque, tomb, and educational complex dedicated to him in downtown Tanta. The most colorful and famous of the annual celebrations is the autumn **mawlid** or birthday festival, attended mostly by working-class Egyptians, especially farmers, from all over the country.

It is noteworthy that Sayyid al-Badawī's biggest celebration is held according to the pre-Islamic solar and not the lunar Muslim calendar. Ancient Egyptians worshiped the sun and gave a religious interpretation to the agricultural round of the seasons, which marked not only the progress of the heavenly bodies through the skies but also the waxing and waning of the life-giving Nile River, whose yearly inundation brought the essential silt and water upon which Egypt's life depended absolutely in premodern times. The solar, rather than the Islamic lunar, dating of the greatest of the saint's celebrations suggests a pre-Islamic antecedent for the festival, as do the folk practices long associated with the autumn *mawlid*, which include magical charms to induce fertility in women. Also, the autumn event features extensive market activities centering in agricultural products and related goods.

Sayyid Aḥmad al-Badawī lived during the period when Sufi brotherhoods, *ṭarīqas*, were being established throughout the *Umma*. As a youth, Sayyid al-Badawī had been a famous pugilist and horseman, but after a period of residence in Mecca, he took up serious studies in Islamic sciences and went on to advanced Sufi meditation in his travels to visit Sufi masters in Iraq and Syria, together with his brother. Arriving at Tanta, he was at first resisted by the local Sufis, but after a while he established a secure place and a reputation for strange and unsettling spiritual exercises. Sayyid al-Badawī's former renown as a martial arts expert continued to color the perceptions of his followers as well as his cautious detractors, so that his cult developed into a following of the more humble, down-to-earth levels of society. This saint is a sort of god among Egypt's saints, and the common folk sense Sayyıd al-Badawī's presence everywhere and are thus extremely careful about how they refer to him in conversation.

Although the Badawī complex of veneration and lore contains large amounts of folk material unrelated to either Qur'ān or Sunna, let alone to official theological and legal interpretations, there is a strong connection with Sunnī orthopraxy through the respected theological school attached to the mosque-tomb complex in Tanta. The great Egyptian Muslim theologian Muḥammad 'Abduh (1849–1905) was educated at the Tanta institute, as have been other prominent Islamic leaders.

Egypt's tolerance toward folk beliefs and practices among its Muslim multitudes indicates a confident attitude toward life's complexities, a national trait that can be traced to ancient times when the Nile people worshiped all kinds of deities and incorporated them into a harmonious if, to modern people, baroque hierarchy of animals, monsters, hybrid creatures, divinized humans, elemental forces, and moral virtues. Muslim saints in Egypt continue the old pattern of hierarchy by the popular practice of seeking intercession with God through them.

Intercession is believed by Muslim scholars to be permitted through the Prophet Muḥammad when Judgment Day comes; that is, Muḥammad will intercede on behalf of Muslims directly with God for their forgiveness. But most official Muslim authorities agree that there is little if any scriptural basis for the intercession of saints. Nevertheless, people do in fact seek such intercession in many ways. They do not consider this to be idolatrous in the least. Rather, they view the friendly help of a holy personage as a natural link between humans and God, a sort of exemplary proof of God's providence and continuous working in the world for their ultimate good. The holiness of Muslim saints thus does not inhere in persons as such, but in the blessings and power bestowed on them by God, which are then mediated outward to needy human devotees.

Since the stern puritanical reforms of the Wahhābi movement got under way in Arabia more than two hundred years ago, saint veneration has been outlawed in the Hijāz and all regions under the authority of the Sa'udi dynasty. But neighboring Yemen has continued to maintain extensive saint cults at the popular level of culture. And in Southern Asia, North Africa, the Fertile crescent, and Indonesia, varieties of saint veneration are found, sometimes in profusion.

In North Africa, saint veneration is closely linked with family lineages and political power. Each major tribal grouping expresses its prestige and cohesion as a potent sociopolitical entity through its sacred sites, where its saints, called marabouts, are buried. Not all marabouts are dead, whether in Egypt or Morocco; they serve as sacred resources for people seeking intercession, boons, healing, and other blessings. A marabout is a saint who has been identified because of wonder working, descent from the Prophet Muḥammad, or both. The word marabout itself has a relationship with military defense of the Muslim community, because *murābiṭs* (the Arabic source of "marabout") were medieval warriors who guarded the frontiers of the Islamic lands in fortified positions. The word *murābiṭ* means "one who is bound" to something; in the case of Moroccan holy men with this title, they are bound to God.

The phenomenon of saint veneration in Morocco and North Africa is generally linked with Sufism, as well as with tribal, clan, and family groupings. Sufism and sainthood are also closely tied in other Muslim countries, such as Pakistan and India. But way over at the other end of the Islamic world from Morocco is a major Muslim region where Sufism has relatively little influence, but where the veneration of God's friends is nevertheless practiced, too. Let us look at Indonesian saint veneration.

The "Nine Saints" of Java

Java was Islamized, according to legends, by nine holy men who brought the teachings of the Qur'ān to that island in the fifteenth and sixteenth centuries. They are known collectively in Javanese as the *wali songo*, or "nine saints." Although these heroes are historically connected in some respects with Sufism and although Sufi merchants and travelers were prominent in spreading Islam peacefully throughout the Malay-Indonesian archipelago, the *wali songo* tradition is not limited to Sufism. In fact, Sufism of the *Ṭarīqa* variety, with established brotherhoods and extensive lineages and linkages throughout the islands, never became as firmly entrenched in Indonesia as in Egypt, Iraq, North Africa, and the Indian subcontinent, where it has sometimes dominated. In Indonesia, it could be said that the indigenous tradition, deeply influenced by pre-Islamic Javanese, Hindu, and Buddhist beliefs and practices, was already so profoundly mystical in orientation that Sufism was superfluous. In other words, the Javanese especially were converted to Islam not as to the strange new worldview of Semitic monotheism, but as to a familiar path of shared mystical convictions already held in essence by pre-Islamic Indonesians.

One of the nine Indonesian saints was Sunan Ampel, who established Islam at Ampel in East Java near the modern city of Surabaya. This *walī's* original name was Raden ("Prince") Rahmat, the son of an Arab missionary in Champa. After his successes as a missionary on the north coast of East Java, he came to be venerated as the leading Muslim saint of Java and was given the title by which he has been remembered in his cult: Sunan Ampel, "Prince of Ampel." The large mosque-tomb complex dedicated to the memory of Sunan Ampel and a number of other great *walīs* in the old quarter of Surabaya is the scene of a variety of religiously oriented activities, like Arabic and Qur'ānic instruction, Friday congregational worship, religious education, community services, and youth activities. The surrounding streets are residential and commercial with religious bookstores, sellers of incense, perfumes, souvenirs, and other items standard near Friday mosques in all parts of the Muslim world. There are many old Arab families in the Ampel district and the casual stroller can hear Arabic as well as the native Indonesian and Javanese being spoken in conversation in some of the shops, especially those catering to buyers of classical Islamic texts in Arabic. In fact, the "feel" of the Ampel district is very much like the atmosphere of the medieval Azhar district in Cairo, with its venerable mosque and university, kiosks, religious bookstores, and bazaar. Women dress with modest Islamic covering of the hair, arms, and legs, while men often wear caps such as those found in other Muslim countries of southern and Southeast Asia.

The most notable times at Ampel are when religious festivals are held, as in the fasting month of Ramaḍān, when evenings are given over to joyful group recitation and people fill the narrow streets shopping and socializing in family and neighborhood groups. A very special time is when the saint's birthday is celebrated with a *mawlid*, just as in Egypt and other places. Religious organizations parade through the streets with flags and banners, and men and boys chant sacred songs in honor of Sunan Ampel. The old walled-in graveyard next to the main mosque fills with pilgrims and local pious people, the men and boys at one end and the women and girls at the other, both groups facing the central area where the saint reposes in a fenced-in plot together with a number of fellow saints. The *imām* of the mosque and other officials and dignitaries spend periods leading a multitude in reciting long litanies together, calling down blessings on the Prophet Muḥammad and recalling the heroic work of Sunan Ampel and other Muslim missionaries to Java.

On one of the days of the *mawlid* there is a group circumcision of little boys, a standard feature of saint festivals in Java, commemorated in modern times by a "class" photo. Circumcision is a genuine rite of passage when it occurs near adolescence, as it often does in Southeast Asia. The boys are first brought to a clinic and given a medical examination. Later they are operated on, with their parents and relatives seated nearby under a canopy. There is much joy and

Women and children at the mawlid *of Sunan Ampel, Surabaya, East Java, meditating and reciting litanies near the saint's tomb.*

children running around, except for those about to be circumcised. They are set apart and have some dread of the ordeal, but their new status afterwards normally more than makes up for the pain and anxiety suffered both during the operation and in the time leading up to it.

The *mawlid* of Sunan Ampel in Surabaya is a major Indonesian saint day, but it does not compare with the Tanta *mawlid* of Sayyid Aḥmad al-Badawī either in scale or prestige or in the variety of folk-magical associations and practices around its fringes. Sunan Ampel is still a major Indonesian Muslim saint, but other regions of Java venerate other of the nine *walīs* so that in Tuban, west of Surabaya, there is a *mawlid* in honor of Sunan Ampel's son, the great *walī* Sunan Bonang, and in nearby Gresik the people visit the hill where Sunan Giri, the great warrior saint who defeated the Hindu armies in the name of Islam is buried. And there are still other saints in Kudus, Demak, and other Javanese locales who command the respect and veneration of continuing cults. Nevertheless, Sunan Ampel does attract visitors from afar. One night, while we were listening to Qur'ān recitation in the graveyard of the Ampel mosque, a teenager with a pack came and sat next to me and my friend and, before falling asleep in that holy place, told us that he had just arrived from central Java after walking and hitchhiking for two days. He had come especially to pay his respects to Sunan Ampel during his *mawlid.*

Shī'ite Saint Veneration

The saint veneration activities described so far are taken from Sunnī contexts and traditions. The Shī'ites have their own holy personages connected with the Prophet's family and the lineage of *Imāms* and their associates. Unlike Sunnī Islam, Shī'ite tradition accords the visitation of the burial places of its sacred heroes a central place within the total belief and practice system. That is, although Shī'ites consider the *Ḥajj* to be one of the Pillars of their religion along with their fellow Sunnī Muslims, they also universally recommend pilgrimages to Karbalā' and the tomb of the martyr Ḥusayn; to Najaf, where the grave of 'Alī, the first *Imām*, reposes; and to other places like Mashhad in eastern Iran, the burial place of the eighth *Imām*, 'Alī Riḍā. A linkage between Shī'ite visitation of the graves of the *Imāms* and the Meccan *Ḥajj* is the practice of visiting the tomb of 'Alī, in Najaf, before continuing on to Mecca for the *Ḥajj*.

There are many features surrounding the Shī'ites' visits to their holy places that are like saints' festivals among Sunnīs, such as popular local practices, Qur'ān chanting in the evenings, buying and selling of things (particularly religious goods), special foods, gatherings of Sufi brotherhoods, and the like. But the Shī'ites have an additional observance that occurs on the fateful tenth day of the month of Muḥarram, the anniversary of the tragic martyrdom of Ḥusayn, son of 'Alī and grandson of the Prophet, in Karbalā', back in 680. Remember that Ḥusayn, together with his close kin and supporters, was on the way to Iraq to accept leadership of the Shī'ites there, in preparation for an attempted recovery of rule of the *Umma* from the Damascus-based Umayyad dynasty. Ḥusayn was intercepted by the caliphal forces at Karbalā' and, after being warned to desist from his course, upon refusing was cut down along with his followers. The women and children were transported in bonds to the capital, Damascus.

The commemoration of this black day in Shī'ite sacred history is a "passion play," called **ta'zīya**, "consolation," which recounts the events and their meaning. *Ta'zīya* productions are mounted in Iran, Iraq, Pakistan, India, and wherever Shī'ites live. Sometimes they are held in special theatres, sometimes in town squares or other places. In small villages storytellers unfurl cartoon-like paintings of the Karbalā' story while singing and reciting the episodes as the gathered audience shares in all the emotions generated by the tragedy and becomes, in a sense, part of the long-ago saga as it is ritually recalled and incorporated into the ongoing experience of Shī'ites. For example, when a Shī'ite soldier falls on the field of battle, he is identified with Ḥusayn. At the end of the year, when Shī'ites in Iran remember their dead of the year, a close, intentional identification with Ḥusayn is made. In the case of women, the identification is often with Ḥusayn's mother, Fātima, who also died young.

Ḥusayn long ago became the prototype of the suffering righteous person, whose wounds would be used by God to redeem the Shī'ites if they sustained their faith and dedication to what they consider to be true Islam. The martydrom of Ḥusayn and the ritual repetitions of it by means of the *ta'zīya* sacred drama are finally not tragic at all; rather, they are a persistent showing forth of victorious faith in God's ultimate vindication, similar to the expression of the battered and humiliated Old Testament figure Job, who declared during his lowest point, "I know that my Redeemer lives, and that on the latter day he will stand upon the earth."

According to tradition, the severed head of Ḥusayn was first transported to Damascus, the capital of the Umayyads. Later it was moved, according to another tradition, to Cairo by the Shī'ite Fatimids who founded the city in 969. There is a large mosque dedicated to Ḥusayn near the Azhar University in Cairo and it is believed that among its treasured relics is Ḥusayn's head. Many miracles have been attributed to Ḥusayn, as well as marvels associated with his birth, death, and accomplishments. His head is said to have emitted a wonderful perfume in one legend, and in another to have recited Qur'ānic passages.

During the *ta'zīya* performance Ḥusayn is always dressed in a green tunic which is worn under his white grave shroud, the latter symbolizing martydom. Green has always been associated with Muḥammad and is thus the Islamic color par excellence. Descendants of the Prophet are permitted to wear green turbans, symbolizing their

Ta'zīya *performance in a special theatre designed for the Shī'ite "passion play" in Shiraz, Iran. The mounted actor represents the Imām Ḥusayn, just before his martyrdom at Karbalā' in 680* C.E. *(Photo used by permission of Peter J. Chelkowski.)*

status as *sayyids*. The Umayyad commander in the *ta'zīya* wears red, symbolizing conflict and bloodshed, the color of the enemies of the Shī'ites.

The Muslim Life Cycle: Rites and Processes

We have seen how Qur'ān recitation and saint veneration work to reinforce and integrate Islamic beliefs and values, the first by constant reminding of God's transcending authority expressed in a message and a powerful spiritual presence, the second through sanctification of specific persons in particular places, showing divine providence percolating, as it were, through the soil of ordinary life. In this final section we shall see how Islamic beliefs and values are expressed in the behavioral patterns associated with the major transitions of human life.

Islamic behavior, whether the official practices prescribed as the Pillars of Islam or variable rituals of social relations and etiquette, comprise a complex code regulating individual and communal life at different levels. This code sets Muslims apart from other peoples and religions. Although Muslims warmly welcome and embrace new members into the *Umma*, they do so with the utmost regard for those individuals becoming new kinds of persons with Islamic convictions and habits.

Life cycle stages are points at which both the structure and dynamics of Muslim life intersect. All cultures have rites of passage from one stage to another, whether they occur primarily in the religious sphere, along social, civil, military, or political lines, or combinations of these, as is most common. For example, an Australian aboriginal puberty rite of coming of age included spiritual and social dimensions in an integrated whole: to be considered mature and responsible enough to share in the sacred wisdom of the tribe's origins carried with it a significant portion in the guardianship of the wisdom in the future. The knowledge of sacred origins in Australian aboriginal society was a principal element in being a complete human and thus a trusted member of the community as well as a spiritually fulfilled person.

Islam does not have a formal rite of passage for entry into its ranks. An individual desiring to become a Muslim has only to utter the *Shahāda* ("There is no god but God; Muḥammad is the messenger of God") with a sincere heart to join the *Umma*. Normally the witnessing is done in the presence of other Muslims, and that is recommended; but one may submit alone in the presence of God. By the time one actually joins his or her fellow Muslims, for example in the performance of the *Ṣalāt*, one will again utter the *Shahāda* periodically. The witnessing in the *Shahāda* is not itself the conversion, but the public expression of it.

However, once a person has become a Muslim, then all of the duties as well as privileges of membership in the *Umma* are immediately in force. It is normal for an uncircumcised adult male convert to Islam to undergo circumcision. Most converts also take an Islamic name, which may simply be added to previous names or used as a replacement name. In either case, a significant statement is made about the person's new identity as a Muslim. Preferred names among Muslims are 'Abdullāh ("Servant of God"), 'Abdurraḥmān ("Servant of the Merciful"), Muḥammad, 'Alī, 'Ā'isha, Fāṭima, Khadīja, Ḥasan, Ḥusayn, 'Umar, and other names associated with the Prophet's family and companions. Two well-known Americans adopted Muslim names upon conversion: boxer Cassius Clay became Muhammad Ali and basketball player Lew Alcindor became Kareem Abdul Jabbar.

Birth and Childhood

Islamic rites of passage begin at birth and continue to death and even beyond. When a Muslim couple engage in marital relations, they first utter the **Basmala**, "In the Name of God the Merciful, the Compassionate." Upon the birth of a child, someone recites the call to prayer in the infant's ear. The seventh day is the traditional time for naming, as well as a related ceremony consisting of the sacrifice of an animal and the shaving of a tuft of the baby's hair. When a child begins to talk, simple Islamic words and phrases are taught, like the *Basmala*. As soon as possible, training in reading and reciting the Qur'ān is begun. Young boys and girls may play together, but unrelated males and females are separated as puberty approaches.

Puberty and Circumcision

Coming of age rites among Muslims vary considerably from region to region, but circumcision of boys, although it often is performed long before puberty, is a universal symbol of Muslim male identity. In some regions, girls are "circumcized," too, by scarring or even excision of the clitoris, but this operation is largely a pattern of culture and not a religious rite. Circumcision of boys is often performed in infancy, but many undergo the operation around age seven, and significant numbers experience it at the onset of puberty. In the last case, circumcision is often associated with a first complete recitation of the Qur'ān. A double potency is thus proclaimed: knowledge of God's teaching, which enables the person to distinguish between right and wrong, and biological as well as cultural male potency as a full-fledged Muslim and "citizen" of the *Umma*, with full enjoyment of its privileges and responsibility for its defense and propagation.

To return to the observation that Islam requires no rites of passage into its ranks, it is sufficient simply to cite the rites surrounding birth, childhood, and puberty to discern a processual dimension to a person's development as a complete human being within the Islamic scheme of things. That is, Muslim life is a dynamic, developmental process of *becoming*. Because Islam is a complete way of life, as Muslims so often emphasize, there have to be accompanying rites that mark and reinforce the *natural* cycles of human life in Islamic ways. All humans typically are born, develop, mature, pass through a marriageable phase when reproduction is a possibility, grow old, and die. All societies have rites marking these transitions. Islam puts its special stamp on each of these natural passages and thus consecrates them to God in a manner that recalls our discussion of the original constitution or *fiṭra* of human existence as a good creation, made from the beginning for the service of God. We turn now to two of the greatest transitions in human life: marriage and death.

Marriage

Islamic marriage is a time for great rejoicing and celebration. In traditional settings, which are dominant still in most Muslim regions, the parents serve as matchmakers. Young women are not allowed to go out looking for a husband, although they may express their preferences and they have the right to refuse someone selected for them. A man may initiate the matchmaking, but he normally does not approach a prospective bride directly. Propriety and custom require indirect negotiations with the woman's father or other male guardian. The betrothed pair are not permitted to be alone together before marriage, although they may sometimes enjoy each other's company in the presence of other responsible adults such as parents.

Islamic law has strict regulations concerning relations between the sexes. The concept of **maḥram** refers to the permitted degrees of close blood relationship within which males and females may not marry and thus may associate socially with each other. A proper Muslim woman never associates socially with a non-*maḥram* male. Even in cases of necessity there is usually another close adult relative in attendance, such as in visits to the doctor or other places where outside contact with the opposite sex is unavoidable. In modern settings such as Western universities it is generally acceptable for Muslim female students, for example, to confer with their male professors one on one in the professional setting of a faculty office. But such a situation is an exception, bowing to the custom of the host country; all other Islamic standards of deportment are otherwise observed.

There are no prohibitions regarding socialization between females with each other or males with other males. This leads to a two-sided, but not divided, society among Muslims. For example, when unrelated Muslims meet for a meal, the custom is for the women to occupy separate rooms and eat together, while the men associate only with each other. Proper Muslim men do not normally inquire about female members of a non-kinsman's family, although it is expected that a general inquiry about the well-being of the *family as a whole* be offered. Thus, the society is not divided, essentially; it is simply most fully articulated at the *family* level where the division of roles, labor, and responsibility between husband and wife, boys and girls, uncles and aunts, and so forth exhibits a basic complementarity rather than opposition.

The Qur'ān permits Muslim men to marry up to four wives concurrently, provided all are treated equally. Since this is a practical difficulty—many would say impossibility—there is a wide consensus that marriages should be monogamous except in special circumstances (as, for example, in early Islamic and other times when there was a surplus of women, because of high death rates of men in battle). Women are permitted only one spouse at a time. Divorce is allowed for both partners, but it is generally easier for the man to dissolve the marriage. Muslim men may marry non-Muslim women, so long as they are from the People of the Book, that is Jews or Christians, but Muslim women are not permitted to marry non-Muslim men. Conversion of the male to Islam is always a possibility; however, if it is done solely to remove the legal disqualification such conversion is disapproved.

The marriage ceremony is a simple affair of writing up and signing a contract between the partners. There is no specific ritual connected with the ceremony, at least as a requirement, although it is customary for someone to recite a passage of the Qur'ān and to deliver a brief inspirational speech. At the signing of the contract, the groom meets with a male representative of the bride. An official from the government often supervises the proceedings, although he does not do so in any sense like a cleric; his responsibility is merely legal.

It is after the legal ceremony of signing that the real marriage festivities begin. These celebrations vary widely according to region, but all Muslims consider it important to launch the marriage with a happy time for relatives and other guests to the extent that means and circumstances permit. This typically includes special and abundant food, new clothes, Qur'ān recitation by a hired professional, music, dancing (folk types prevail, with each sex dancing together), bright lights and decoration, dramatic performances (e.g., shadow puppetry in Java), and other things. Sometimes the festivities continue for days. There may occasionally be mischievous snooping on the newlyweds, but in good fun. In Middle Eastern societies there is still found the ritual exhibition of a bloody sheet after the marriage has been consummated, thus certifying the propriety of the union and preserving the honor of the virginal bride's family as well as demonstrating the virility of the groom.

Death and Its Rites

At the approach of death, the dying person should turn her or his face toward Mecca and say, "There is no god but God," in preparation for the questioning that is believed to occur in the tomb by the angels of death. The thirty-sixth *sūra* of the Qur'ān is often recited to the dying person, after death, and at funeral and memorial observances, because it summarizes so vividly the end of life and the passage to the hereafter. "Who will revive these bones when they have rotted away? Say: He will revive them Who produced them at the first, for He is Knower of every creation." (36:77—78).

After death the deceased's body must receive its final ablution, which is a complete ritual bath performed according to precise rules. No embalming is permitted, but the body may be scented before it is wrapped in a plain white grave cloth that completely enfolds the corpse. It is not necessary to place the corpse in a coffin. Islamic law requires that the burial be performed the same day as the death if possible, but burial may not take place after sundown.

It is a communal obligation to follow the funeral procession to the burial place, but it is sufficient that only a representative group actually do it. The funeral *Ṣalāt*, consisting of four parts in each of which "God is most great!" is uttered, is performed at the gravesite with all standing throughout. It is even possible to perform the *Ṣalāt* in the absence of the corpse. When the burial party arrives at the gravesite, the first *sūra* of the Qur'ān is recited. If it has not been done earlier, the person presiding at the burial whispers the *Shahāda* into the ear of the deceased just before beginning to fill in the grave, so as to remind the departed one of the true religion and the correct answer to the questioning angels waiting to receive the dead soul. The traditional and recommended grave is four to six feet deep, with a shelf hollowed out on one side. The corpse is placed on this shelf, with the head turned toward Mecca.

There is strong evidence in the *ḥadīth* that excessive mourning and loud lamentation cause the deceased to suffer in the grave. The best expression of grief and respect for the dead is recitation of the Qur'ān, whose merit redounds to the benefit of the deceased. After the day of burial there is usually a reception in commemoration of the death. In Egypt, for example, an observance is held on the fortieth day after the death, where people express their condolences and stay a while to sip coffee and listen to Qur'ān recitation.

The Muslim martyr does not need to receive the final ablution because his or her wounds are purification in the sight of God, who rewards the fallen warrior with immediate admission to paradise. Nor is the funeral *Ṣalāt* said over the martyr's remains. It is interesting to observe that persons considered martyrs are not limited to those who die in battle defending Islam. The pilgrim who dies while making the *Ḥajj* is a martyr, as is one who perishes while reciting the Qur'ān or engaged in other pious acts.

Conclusions

We have reviewed only the bare essentials of Islamic rites of passage connected with the life cycle. Other rites of passage attend initiation into a Sufi brotherhood, which typically culminates in the bestowing of the patched frock, symbol of the spiritual poverty of the Sufi dervish. Other symbols may also accompany the status change from novice to adept on the Sufi way, such as the gift of a cap or the placing of the disciple's hand into that of his master so that the latter's *baraka* may be transmitted, thus extending the lineage one link further.

Titles are also part of status changes in Islam. The title of *Ḥājjī*, "pilgrim," has already been mentioned. The title *shaykh* is applied to various types of Muslims, from the youth who has just completed memorizing the Qur'ān to any older man who is respected for devotion and religious learning, even if not as a professional scholar. In Iran, the title *ayatollah*, which literally means "sign of God," has in modern times been bestowed on exceptionally pious and learned religious scholars with significant followings. The famous Ayatollah Khomeini, leader of Iran's Islamic revolutionary government, is but one of thousands of venerated religious guides in Iran today who bear the title of *ayatollah*.

In Java many Muslims observe Islamic rites of passage such as circumcision and marriage by sponsoring the performance of a classical shadow puppet play. The traditional stories that are dramatized by the manipulation of leather puppets against a white screen are taken from Hindu myth and epic, but they are thought to have enduring meaning and power within the Javanese worldview as interpreted in an Islamic framework. In such classical Javanese regions as Yogyakarta and Solo in central Java the majority of guests, especially of more well-to-do hosts, expect a marriage especially to be celebrated by a suitably opulent expression of traditional high culture such as shadow plays and accompanying gamelan music provide. It is relevant, also, that the puppet master is a person of high ritual status within the Javanese value system. Thus, a proper Islamic marriage—which, remember, does not in itself require anything beyond the basic contract signing—when joined to a traditional Javanese festive structure produces a dynamic that fulfills both what God has commanded and what the Javanese themselves have inherited as an ancient legacy of *the way things are done*.

Islam as a Dynamic Reality

The preceding chapter focused on structures of Islam and the Muslim life, with special emphasis on the Pillars, the Qur'ān and Sunna, the *Sharī'a*, and Sufism. This chapter has examined dynamics of Muslim life beyond the formal structures of orthoprax prescription and precept. The Arabic word *islām* is itself a verbal noun containing within its meaning a dynamic sense of "submitting" and not an objectified sense of "submission" as a kind of static entity; that is, Muslims must *intend* submission and all the accompanying attitudes and acts that make up Muslim being in the world, each day. Just as a single act of repentance, for Muslims, is not a once-for-all guarantee of success, so also must surrender to God be that lifelong process of becoming that was described in our discussion of life cycle. Muḥammad, when asked whether he, a great prophet, had ever felt the need to repent, to turn again toward God, declared once that he repented seventy times each day. Likewise, Islam is a constant turning again in submission to God, requiring the patterns and structures of doctrine and devotion as a clearly marked path for what, after all, is a journey through life in which human will in history is progressively harmonized with that preexisting, life-sustaining *fiṭra* that is humankind's birthright.

Although this chapter has attempted to show how the Qur'ān contributes to the dynamics of Muslim individual and community life, nothing has been said about the Prophet's Sunna. But Muḥammad's teaching and example are of fundamental importance in the teaching of Qur'ānic interpretation and recitation, as well as the learning of how to enjoy as well as follow the Qur'ān in life's varied situations. Similarly, the veneration of saints derives much from the anciently developed practices surrounding the veneration of Muḥammad. The Prophet's birthday is celebrated in most Muslim countries by colorful festivities, thereby serving as a universal saint's day, which then is mirrored in multifarious forms by the *mawlids* of saints from Morocco to Java, all of which pay respects in some manner to Muḥammad, the greatest saint of all.

The Muslim life cycle rites are all in some way also based on Muḥammad's or the Qur'ān's teaching. For example, circumcision is not prescribed in the Qur'ān, but it is mentioned in the *ḥadīth* literature, from which it received its high status among the marks of Muslim identity. In general, it should be remembered that the Qur'ān teaches Muslims *what* to believe and do, whereas the Sunna prescribes and describes *how* faith is to be incorporated into all dimensions of life. As in life Muḥammad and the Qur'ān were practically indistinguishable, so also since has the Prophet's charisma become progressively transferred onto the Muslim community itself. Thus the *Umma* is also a charismatic reality, bearing both God's message and his Prophet's exemplary teaching not primarily by means of written records, but through the ingrained convictions, attitudes, and habits of persons in a strong communal bond. Islamic structure and dynamics come together when Qur'ān and Sunna are thus internalized by Muslims.

CHAPTER V

Islam in Today's World

The recent emergence of a renewed and vigorous Islam was noted toward the end of chapter II. The strength of Islam in today's world may be witnessed in several areas: political expression, economics, the rejection of Western and materialistic values, the acceptance of science and technology, and widespread missionary activities on a global scale.

Muslim Rejection of the West

It may seem contradictory to mention together the rejection of Western values and the acceptance of science and technology, because the latter have been dominated by Western peoples or at least most of the approaches and patterns of inquiry have been developed in the modern West. Nevertheless, Muslims share the memory that in earlier times their civilization made great progress in science, especially in such fields as mathematics, medicine, astronomy, geography, and optics. For various reasons, the Islamic world fell behind in scientific inquiry. The fact that the West succeeded in developing modern science in no way suggests that it was because of a better religion or more intelligent human resources. Rather, historical, political, economic, and geographical circumstances permitted the West to monopolize science and industrial technology.

The problem with the West's domination of science and technology according to Muslim critics is that underneath it is a materialistic worldview that denies the sovereignty of God and any covenant responsibility from his human creatures. What is more, Muslim reformers agree that Western materialism seduces people to a blind consumerism based on satisfaction of sensual desires. In the contemporary world of global communications and markets, non-Western peoples are also victimized by Western commercial exploitation of universal human cravings of a hedonistic sort. Thus, we find in stricter Islamic circles a rejection of rock and other popular music, alcohol, social mixing of the sexes, motion pictures, Western television series, bank interest, pornography, and other things.

But Muslims endorse many other products of Western technology and marketing strategies like automobiles, airplanes, medicine, industrial manufacturing, computers, electronic media, and especially technical education. North American and European universities and technical institutes have large enrollments from Asian and African countries, including significant numbers of Muslim students from nations like Saudi Arabia, Kuwait, the Gulf Emirates, Pakistan, Egypt, Iran, Lebanon, Syria, Malaysia, and Indonesia. The largest number of foreign nationals in European, Australian, and North American universities is from Malaysia, a country that is 50 percent Muslim.

The rejection of Western materialism on the part of many vocal Muslim critics is not shared by all or even most Muslims. For one thing, the characterization of the West as "materialistic" needs to be placed in perspective, because there is much religious belief and ferment in Western countries, too. And Western criticisms of materialism are strong and sophisticated, extending beyond consumerism to assessments of and attacks on ideological materialism, whether Marxist or capitalist. Religious people everywhere—Muslim, Christian, Buddist, Hindu—share important insights and convictions about the human condition and the permissibility of attachment to material goods and the proper disciplining of human passions. In the Islamic case, rejection of what are regarded to be Western values and ways has less to do with the West than with forming and maintaining Islamic allegiances. The memories of Western colonialism and imperialism are bitter, and the descendants of the colonized peoples, including many of those in Muslim countries, are committed to ensuring that foreign domination does not recur, whether in political and economic or in more subtle symbolic, cultural, and social ways. Islamic convictions and ordering principles are believed by many to be the strongest bulwark against foreign domination.

The traditional separation of the world into the *Dār al-Islām* and the *Dār al- Ḥarb* may be seen in today's world in the rejection of the

West as a religious duty. Materialism and consumerism are regarded by staunch Muslims as forms of idolatry. But exploitation of the natural world by means of science and technology is considered not only permissible but encouraged by God, so long as it is done according to Islamic principles that are adumbrated, if not specifically detailed, in the Qur'ān and Sunna. *Ijtihād* becomes once again an important method of relating God's Word to the world in the present day when so many new developments and discoveries need to be evaluated.

More extremist Islamic revolutionary movements call for a total removal of Western and especially American interests and influences from Islamic nations. This rejection sometimes takes the form of *jihād*, in the sense of actual holy warfare, which increasingly includes terrorism. Although most Muslims do not endorse terrorism, powerful emotions are stirred among them when extremist groups carry out their aims in the name of Islam. Islam thus serves both as religion and ideology, that is, a means of relating to God in faith and service and a means of mobilizing fellow humans for political and social ends. Islam is co-opted for many reasons in this process, but overall Islam may serve as a symbol for otherwise highly diverse peoples who have in common a deep-seated aversion to outside agencies thought to be responsible for their current plight, whether injustice and revolution in Lebanon, the Israeli occupation of Palestine, a pro-Western government in Egypt, or the Soviet occupation of Afghanistan. In revolutionary Iran, where Western influences have been systematically uprooted, the West nevertheless continues to serve as the primary symbol of satanic evil, partly because it helps the rulers maintain a grip on their people.

Islam and Muslims in the West

We have witnessed conflicting opinions on what results from close contacts with Western peoples and institutions. On the one side is the view that exposure to Western ways corrupts and turns Muslims from the Straight Path. It is true, for example, that Muslim youth who attend Western universities find themselves in strange social situations with little or no reinforcement of their accustomed social patterns, which include close family ties, no mixing of the sexes, and well-imprinted patterns of ritual observance. Western daytime work and class schedules do not immediately make way for prayer times, nor is the Ramaḍān fast thought to be conducive to efficiency and productivity. But often foreign Muslim students in the West seek each other out, if not for religious, then for cultural and language reasons: Malaysians, Indonesians, and Bangladeshis tend to form support systems, as do Arabs and Iranians. (Often Muslim students of diverse nationalities cooperate in forming student associations and observing *Ṣalāt* and other duties.) In our experience, Muslim visitors to the United States, for example, sharply distinguish their own values and customs from the prevailing ethos and adjust accordingly, accepting what they can and maintaining their own ways as far as possible.

Muslim visitors in the West tend to become stronger Muslims rather than straying into alien ways. For one thing, North American and European societies have free presses and a high degree of freedom of association and expression that tolerates dissenting and even radical viewpoints. Muslims and others from the East are able to form associations and express opinions that would be forbidden and even severely punished in their native countries. So, ironically, while Muslim students in the West benefit from its superior scientific and technological education, they also discipline themselves in religious ways, including witnessing to their convictions through **da'wa**, the missionary "call" to outsiders to enjoy the benefits of Islam.

There is no question but that Muslim degree earners, when they return to their countries, carry with them a wide range of reactions and attitudes concerning Western and non-Muslim ways. But a significant number of Muslims remain in Western countries, for economic betterment, professional opportunities, and other reasons. The presence of these people has brought about the first significant development of Islamic institutions in the West. Muslims comprise the second largest religious community in France now, way behind the Roman Catholics, but ahead of the Protestants. There are significant Muslim communities in Germany and the United Kingdom, too, as well as in the Netherlands. In Canada, the Muslim population is well established, especially in major cities. And in the United States there are as many as three million Muslims now. Very significant is the increase of Muslim conversions, so that gradually Western Muslim communities will cease to be largely ethnic enclaves but will increasingly become native to their regions, peacefully coexisting with other religious communities, especially Christians and Jews. The following case study illustrates what can happen when a Muslim community has developed a long-term tradition in an American setting.

The Islamic Center of Greater Toledo

The American manufacturing city of Toledo, Ohio, has attracted many peoples from foreign countries to its factories. Among these people were Syrian and Lebanese Muslim immigrants who started arriving around the turn of the century. In the late thirties, a number of families from the Middle East established the Syrian-American Muslim Society. In 1954 Toledo's first Islamic center was erected to provide a place for community worship and other activities. The late sixties and early seventies witnessed an influx of many more Muslims into the Toledo area. The center thus needed much more space, so it was decided to purchase a sizable tract and erect a major building. The site chosen was a pastoral setting at the crossing of two interstate highways, several miles outside Toledo in suburban Perrysburg. The late Turkish-born Toledo architect Talat Itil designed the new structure, which features a large white dome flanked by two 135-foot-tall Turkish style "pencil" minarets. The two-story building has an octagonal prayer room under the dome, a large lecture hall adjacent, plus eight classrooms, a well-stocked and staffed library, offices, a medical clinic, a mortuary, a professional-level kitchen, and a spacious dining hall. Seventy-two custom-designed stained glass windows adorn the building. They feature calligraphic designs drawn from the Qur'ān, written in different styles. The plot of forty-five acres sets off the center nicely, as do the lawns, flower beds, and decorative shrubs and trees. Travelers on the interstate highways are often strongly impressed by the beautiful Indo-Turkish style mosque. Many of them stop for visits, so many that the center has instituted special tours ending with a first-class Middle Eastern luncheon of roast lamb, vegetables, hummus with tahini, tabbouleh and green salads, flat Syrian bread, olives, baklava, and other tasty treats, all at a modest charge. Hospitality is important to Muslims, and the extending of it tells more than words can something of the friendliness and goodwill of the Toledo Muslim community.

Islamic Center of Greater Toledo, near Perrysburg, Ohio.

Activities of the Toledo Islamic Center focus on education, health, social services, youth and recreation, publications, outreach through tours and hospitality, and, most important, worship. The center is open to all Muslims. A council directs the affairs of the center assisted by a board of elders and a ladies auxiliary. Chief officers include a president, a vice-president and general counsel, a secretary, and a treasurer. Administrative and spiritual direction of the center is in the hands of an *imām-director*, who reports to the council. The current *imām* is an Egyptian with thorough classical Islamic training as well as an advanced degree in clinical psychological counseling. He is fluent in English as well as his native Arabic and helps the community maintain a healthy balance between orthodox Islamic training and conduct of life and necessary as well as desirable contacts with American society and values.

There is much that is traditional about the Toledo Islamic Center. The mosque is open daily for prayer, there is a large congregation on Fridays for communal worship, Arabic is taught to some 250 enrolled students, close ties are maintained with other Islamic communities both here and abroad, and the architecture of the main building itself makes a strong statement about origins, aesthetic/symbolic commitments, and pride.

But there are also striking differences between the Toledo community and Muslim communities elsewhere, especially in traditional Islamic societies of the Middle East and Asia. The *Umma* has never known a parish model for religious association. Rather, in Islamic countries, at least, mosques have been made available where needed by the government in cooperation with ministries of religious endowments. Individuals and groups have also erected mosques, but their governance has not been ecclesiastical in style, nor have there been memberships as in Christian parishes. The Islamic Center of Toledo has adapted to the dominant North American pattern of religious sociology by instituting membership, with annual dues that are called "zakat." Moreover, the *imām* of the center is not the highest authority. Rather, he is technically an employee of the council, which is the legally incorporated authority for all center activities and property. The council and board of elders together resemble, respectively, the elders and deacons of Presbyterian church polity. The congregation parallels the Presbyterian session and enjoys the privilege of voting on important issues. But the council, like Presbyterian elders, has supreme authority over the affairs of the center. At this point the analogy with Presbyterian polity breaks down, for in the case of the Toledo Islamic Center there is no official transcendent authority like Presbyterianism's synod and general assembly.

The Islamic Center's peculiar governance structure has not escaped criticism from traditionalist Muslims, mostly from outside America. When outside groups have visited the *imām* and complained about the "un-Islamic" arrangements, he has had to refer them to the council. So far, such confrontations have ended amicably, with deepened understanding of ways in which a community can be truly Islamic and at the same time responsible citizens of an American community. Thus, the Islamic Center of Greater Toledo's innovative approach to polity and governance is considered by its members to be a *bid'a ḥasana*, a "good innovation," and not the type of *bid'a* that is condemned as heresy.

Another unusual aspect of the center's life is the social mixing of the sexes, whether in Sunday School classes (religious education is on Sundays, another common North American Muslim innovation) or at frequent communal luncheons and dinners. When we visited the center and were honored with a special evening dinner, we were frankly amazed to be chatting and laughing around a table with wives, husbands, parents, grandparents, children, and guests from near and far. It was very much like a typical American church supper, except that the food was above average because of the large number of good Lebanese and Syrian cooks. The center's membership includes both Shī'ites and Sunnīs from such countries as Egypt, Lebanon, Syria, Palestine, Turkey, Iraq, Saudi Arabia, Pakistan, India, and thirteen other countries. Occupations include teachers, professors, merchants, doctors, lawyers, realtors, scientists, engineers, contractors, factory workers, laborers, homemakers, and students.

The center members appear to enjoy each other's company greatly through religious education classes, communal meals, worship, special events, and frequent visiting of each other's homes. It appears to us that, whereas in traditional Middle Eastern and Asian countries, Muslim social life centers in constant rounds of visits between members of extended family groups, in the Toledo area members of the Islamic Center extend this circle to include fellow Muslims in mixed social life. Traditional practice of course encourages friendly social visiting outside the family, but it restricts it to groups of the same sex occupying the same social space. For example, when a couple goes to visit unrelated friends in a traditional Muslim setting, the men sit and eat in one part of the house and the women in another. The non-*maḥram* visiting woman may greet the host, but there will be no social interaction beyond that. The same is true of the hostess and the non-*maḥram* male visitor.

What has just been described is the most conservative practice. In actuality, one may encounter Muslim social situations in Pakistan, Indonesia, Malaysia, Egypt, Turkey, and other places where there may be some social mixing of the sexes outside the *maḥram* boundaries. Muslims who mix socially in this way in dominantly Muslim countries are almost always westernized and on the upper social and economic levels. They may be Muslim in the nominal sense only, although it is possible to find modernized (i.e., "westernized") Muslims of deep conviction who nevertheless have a liberal social life-style with circles of friends of both sexes beyond the extended family and beyond the confessional boundaries of Islam.

The striking difference about the Toledo and some other North American Islamic communities is that liberal social mixing is enjoyed within the context of the "parish." In coeducational Sunday School classes, Muslim teenagers discuss the same sorts of issues that Christian and Jewish youth are concerned with, like drugs, rock music and its effects, commitment to God in a world of conflicting values and secularism, growing up, and other things. One of the things that American Muslim youth have to resolve is the tension between wanting to be accepted as normal Americans and at the same time observant Muslims who, with all their liberal habits when compared with traditional Islamic societies, nevertheless cannot in good conscience share in certain aspects of American social life, like dating, dancing, and, at the college level and beyond, drinking alcoholic beverages and choosing an independent sexual life-style.

Another problem faced by all North American Muslims is dietary. Pork is absolutely forbidden and permitted meats must come from animals slaughtered in the proper manner, which, remember, is similar to the Jewish method of koshering food. It is sometimes difficult to avoid pork and pork products in American food, especially prepared varieties. Muslims share a strong repugnance to pork in the American diet. This avoidance is based on divine prohibition, but it has come also to include revulsion at what is believed to be unclean. People who eat pork—the majority of Americans—are in this regard separate from Muslims and somewhat alien. But the same is true of conservative and orthodox Jews, who have an ancient prohibition against pork that extends back long before the coming of Islam. Muslims in diverse places sometimes make a fetish of avoiding pork, while also abstaining from strict observance of Islamic devotional duties and life-style. Somehow, it is apparently believed, the fact that pork is not consumed over one's lifetime mitigates a slack devotional life. This curious observation is mentioned here not in any way to disparage Islam and Muslims, but to demonstrate the power of a negative symbol—in this case avoidance of pork—that reinforces a strong sense of community integrity and belonging.

It is necessary to distinguish among different types of Islamic communities in North America. The Toledo Islamic Center is a diversified community of multiple national backgrounds and contains both Sunnīs and Shī'ites. It is largely middle-and upper-middle-class, and comfortably situated in Middle American life. The members blend into the greater Toledo ambience with their late model cars, suburban homes, American style clothing, and typically American occupations. The women, by and large, do not cover their hair, a mark of Islamic revival that is seen in the behavior of Western converts as much as longstanding Muslims. At a celebration of the second anniversary of the erection of the center and mosque, out-of-town Muslim guests from other American cities stood out in their traditional Islamic garb when compared to the Toledo Muslim women especially, who dressed conservatively, but no more so nor different than well-bred and devout American Jewish or Christian women would in a similar setting. By contrast, at the mosque in Boulder, Colorado, a university city with many international students, Muslim mosque gatherings are strictly separated by sex and the women (whether from abroad or American) cover up completely, leaving only the face and hands exposed.

We do not wish to appear to harp on the dress issue, but it is symbolically significant. The Toledo community seems to be saying by its style that Muslims can and should participate in the dominant American life-style, so long as that does not entail forsaking truly Islamic principles of belief, practice, and comportment. The Boulder Muslim community (and many others like it in North America) appears to be saying by its traditionalist style of community life, including female dress code, that Muslims have a duty to be different when it comes to adhering to their true principles, even if that means significant separations and differences from the dominant social and personal patterns of behavior and dress. There is survival value in maintaining strict Islamic customs. But it may also be true that such pattern maintenance is more easily sustained by a constantly shifting mosque population in a university setting, where Saudis, Kuwaitis, Pakistanis, Malaysians, and other foreign nationals of Muslim belief continually cycle in and out of the community as degrees are earned and new matriculates arrive. Such an Islamic community can maintain over time "pure" Islamic patterns of life and in the bargain provide a comforting and familiar context for foreign Muslim students and others who find American life lonely, bewildering, in some respects disagreeable, and just plain alien.

It is natural for Muslims to gather together wherever they may be. What is more, it is prescribed by their religion to observe the Friday congregational *Ṣalāt* and to come to each other's aid and struggle always to maintain a moral environment. Muslim university students, for example, sometimes find their faith and home ways of life threatened and severely tested by the material wealth and social and intellectual freedom that they experience in the West. Campus Christian groups as well as evangelically minded individuals often seek to convert Muslim students. Proselytization attempts rarely if ever occur in Muslim countries, because they are outlawed by Islam; only *Islamic* missionary endeavors are legal under the *Sharī'a*. Muslims in the *Dār al-Ḥarb* often experience severe disorientation at the sight of a dominant religious presence that is other than Islamic.

Islamic Fundamentalism

The term "fundamentalism" was coined early in this century in an American conservative Protestant framework to characterize a Scripture-based doctrine embracing five key points (the virgin birth of Jesus, his physical resurrection, the infallibility of the Scriptures, the substitutional Atonement, and the physical Second Coming of Christ). The only point with which Muslims agree concerns the infallibility of Scripture—in the Islamic case, of course, the Qur'ān. In recent years it has become popular to refer to conservative militant Muslims as fundamentalists. The name does not quite apply, when taken at its original meaning. But the spirit of Christian fundamentalism is certainly paralleled in Muslim convictions concerning the infallibility of the Qur'ān, literally interpreted, the authentic prophethood of Muhammad as chief and last of the long series of prophets to appear in history, Muhammad's Sunna as impeccable example for human behavior, and the authority of the *Sharī'a* for a closed community of true believers, the *Umma*. Furthermore, Muslims, like evangelical fundamentalist Christians, strenuously apply themselves to the missionary task, believing that it is God's will to convert unbelievers to the true way.

Having demonstrated that there is some justification in applying the term "fundamentalist" in a generic sense to Muslims, it should immediately be added that there is no organizational structure or universally subscribed to creedal statement that binds Muslims together in any formal manner. Nor is there in Protestant Christianity, although for a time such denominations as the Baptists and Presbyterians did contain zealous and disciplined members who adhered to the fundamentalist principles and applied them to their co-religionists as a standard for orthodoxy.

There is a fairly wide range of interpretations and temperament among Muslim individuals and groups that might be content to be called fundamentalist. Some fundamentalists express themselves politically, supporting revolutionary and even terrorist methods, whether against supposed enemies from outside—the West is a frequent target—or against what are deemed to be false or weak individuals and institutions within the *Umma*—Egypt's Anwar Sadat and his regime is a recent example. Other fundamentalists express themselves through preaching, teaching, and other forms of communication, in organizations, schools, universities, mosques, and in print and other media, among which audio-cassette tapes are prominent, because they are easily copied and disseminated, even in countries where the radio or television appearances of certain fundamentalist leaders are outlawed.

A third, broad group of fundamentalist Muslims is found in every region of the world. These are the rank and file believers who are concerned to maintain and hand down as pure a version of the faith as possible. Some of this type are militant in temperament, but not necessarily organized into specific political or cultural groups. Most are moderate, tolerant, and devoutly observant without being especially activist. However, they can be aroused mightily when a threat to the Islamic community and way of life is perceived. I prefer to call this large, centrist group by a name other than fundamentalist. Perhaps the best label is simply "devout Muslim." They all unite around the central beliefs and practices of Islam as contained in Qur'ān and Sunna. This group contains people of all educational levels and occupational groups, rich and poor, men and women, young and old.

Again, all Muslims inhabit at least two cultural spheres, the one providing them with an identity as part of a nation or local ethnic grouping (as Egyptians, or Pakistanis, or Indonesians, or Americans, etc.) and the one providing them with Islamic identity. Sometimes the two are highly contrasting, as in the American context; at other times, as in Arabia, the native cultural context and Islam are closely aligned, because they have coexisted and indeed produced each other. Fundamentalist or devout Muslims—and I do not mean to suggest that the latter is equivalent to the former, although the former surely embraces the latter in significant ways— reflect their cultural backgrounds. The more strongly activist type of fundamentalists generally try to minimize their own cultural idiosyncrasies in favor of a pan-Islamic style of presentation of self, for example, favoring simplicity of clothing and life-style and sometimes verging on asceticism. There is constant mindfulness of following the strict letter of Qur'ān and Sunna and avoiding any compromise of either on the basis of specific cultural background. Such Muslims can move easily from country to country and enjoy a high level of uniformity of comportment, convictions, and goals among their fellow fundamentalists. This unity does not always extend beyond central beliefs, practices, and approved social and personal habits, however. Political and ideological differences can be sharp and the methods preferred to pursue goals can diverge radically.

The key to fundamentalist awareness was forcefully expressed by a Muslim student in a large university class on the Abrahamic religious traditions. When invited to comment on a point the lecturer had made concerning *jihād*, "exertion" in the way of God—which sometimes includes holy warfare—the Malaysian student declared to the class that true Islam is always *jihād*, in every way. He explained that Muslims could not be true to their faith, if they did not see themselves as constantly alert and militant, both as to inward disposition and outward behavior. Both the "lesser" *jihād*—warfare and struggle in the world—and "greater" *jihād*—the continuing exertion against the straying tendencies within us—are absolutely essential to Islam, according to the student. I would say that his focused concern for *jihād* is a mark of fundamentalism everywhere among Muslims.

Some think that Muslim fundamentalism is a view of the world that is generally fearful of change, of newness, specifically of modernity. Recall that the traditional Arabic word for what in English is called "heresy" is *bid'a*, "innovation," in doctrines and practices. But I think that the characterization of Muslim fundamentalism as fearful of change is too negative. It is also misleading, because fundamentalists, or many of them, want radical change: from following Western ways and depending on Western products; from what are perceived to be irreligious and impure "Muslim" leaders and regimes—Sadat and the Shah of Iran are dramatic cases; and what are thought to be idolatrous practices among Muslims, such as visiting saints' tombs for blessings and intercession, paying allegiance to a spiritual guide as in Sufism, and other things.

Backgrounds of the Islamic Revival

Contemporary Muslim fundamentalism has appeared on the world stage in the past few years partly because of the transportation and communications revolutions that have brought the peoples of the earth closer together, both in the various media and in actuality. But the global Islamic revival, which features fundamentalism as a major expression, began well before the current era. The revival can be traced to nineteenth- and twentieth-century reform movements in India, Indonesia, Egypt, Iran, and other places. Even before these movements there was a radical reform in the Arabian Peninsula in the eighteenth century launched by the puritanical preacher Muḥammad ibn ʻAbd al-Wahhāb (c. 1703–1787) and enforced by his protector and collaborator, Ibn Saʻud, ancestor of the present Saʻudi dynasty in Arabia. The Wahhābi movement, as it came to be called, was fanatically opposed to idolatry in any form—physical, symbolic, or psychological. Particularly loathsome was the popular cult of saints in Arabia and elsewhere. It was eradicated from the domains where the Saʻudis and Wahhābis came to dominate, which embraces contemporary Saudi Arabia. As was remarked in the previous chapter, tomb structures were pulled down and all but the plainest and smallest grave markers in cemeteries removed, lest they come to occupy an intermediary place in people's affections and reverence between them and the One God.

Wahhābi reforms spread to Iraq, India, and Africa. One of the key points, in addition to the stamping out of idolatrous practices and beliefs, was the exercise of *ijtihād*, independent legal decision making. For centuries, Sunnī law especially had operated within the context of *taqlīd*, following the decisions and procedures of the early legal experts in a blindly imitative manner. The Wahhābis realized that the Muslims needed to return to the basic sources of inspiration and governance that had created the *Umma* in the beginning and nurtured it during its most creative centuries. This return to Qur'ān, Sunna, and the ways of the early legal experts was a sort of fundamentalism, which has served as a model for subsequent reformers, who have not nevertheless usually followed Wahhābism in all its features, especially its puritanism.

The later nineteenth century saw the rise of Muslim reformers who continued the themes of return to Qur'ān and Sunna, and the repudiation of *taqlīd*, "blind imitation," in law. But certain reformers added something new: a rejection of Western colonialism and a summons to the faithful to rise up and throw off the rule of infidels. The greatest of these revolutionary reformers was Jamāl al Dīn al-Afghānī (1838–1897), a learned and charismatic writer, teacher, orator, and political activist who spread ideas of Islamic reform and liberation from India to Europe. He was especially influential in Egypt, where his assistant, the Egyptian scholar Muḥammad 'Abduh, (1849–1905), continued aspects of Afghānī's work after his death. 'Abduh went on to exert his own long-lasting influence in education, theology, Qur'ān commentary, and legal decision making. 'Abduh reformed the medieval Azhar University in Cairo by liberalizing the curriculum and improving teaching procedures. He urged his fellow Muslims to exploit modern science for Islamic ends, seeing no fundamental contradiction between scientific method and what is taught in the Qur'ān about the nature and scope of human reason and mastery of the things of the natural world.

'Abduh has had strong impacts outside of Egypt, but nowhere more than in Indonesia, where, not long after his death, the young Javanese religious teacher Kiai Hajji Ahmad Dahlan founded a new Muslim movement based on 'Abduh's and modernist Indian teachings. The movement is called Muhammadiyah and it was established as an organization in Yogyakarta in 1912. Muhammadiyah has never been political in focus; rather, it has emphasized educational and social welfare concerns. Many schools were established by the organization, publications launched, and both a women's organization, known as 'Aishiya, and a boy scout movement have been successfully developed. In Indonesia today, Muhammadiyah is still strong, with a vast membership throughout the archipelago. Other, non-Muhammadiyah Indonesians sometimes have characterized the organization as fundamentalist. This is not done in a critical fashion. It simply refers to the strong emphasis among Muhammadiyah Muslims on the Qur'ān and Sunna and the strict practice of the core devotional practices. Traditional Indonesian folk beliefs and practices are rejected in favor of a purified Islam that strives to be in harmony with like-minded Muslims in the rest of the *Umma*. But if fundamentalism connotes rejection of modernity, especially scientific method, technology, and rational thought, then Muhammadiyah is not fundamentalist. My point in selecting Muhammadiyah as an Indonesian version of fundamentalism is to demonstrate how flexible and varied Muslims can be in the pursuit of a purified Islam.

Indonesians are traditionally very tolerant of other Muslims as well as non-Muslims in the interests of harmony, courtesy, and above all, "togetherness," a supreme virtue of these close-knit people, where consensus and mutual responsibility are crucial. In the first chapter I introduced the Indonesian *santris*, who are strictly observant Muslims. The Muhammadiyah people are *santri* in orientation, while the vast majority of Indonesians, especially on Java, are *abangan*, Muslim to be sure, but also dedicated to many aspects of traditional beliefs and practices that existed before the coming of Islam. In fact, most Indonesians are mixtures of different elements, both traditional indigenous and strict Islamic.

In Bangladesh also are "fundamentalists" who are sincere Qur-

The Islamic Foundation Mosque and Garden, Dhaka, Bangladesh.

'ān and Sunna Muslims, but who also pursue philosophical, mystical, and scientific thought. When I first visited Bangladesh, I was told by Western informants that some Muslim scholars I was going to meet were fundamentalists. This was said with a certain foreboding, because of the connotations that militant Muslims have in the press, especially in non-Muslim eyes. But after I had spent some time with the scholars, I soon realized that they had much in common with the rather liberal Muhammadiyah people in Java and other devout Muslim intellectuals elsewhere in Egypt, Pakistan, Iran, and other places.

Whither Islam?

Islam and the Muslim community are thriving in the present age. Their current strength has not been achieved overnight, nor has it been made possible simply by oil wealth in some Muslim nations, although that wealth has had important consequences in aiding the Islamic revival, especially its missionary and educational dimensions. The Wahhābi reform movement, still powerful in its native country, was an entirely indigenous Islamic phenomenon unrelated to Western and non-Muslim concerns and influences. The nineteenth- and early twentieth-century movements did sometimes have rejectionist aspects, but they too relied most heavily on internal resources of Qur'ānic conviction and a strong loyalty and willingness to defend the religion against both internal and external enemies.

The Islamic revival was also greatly extended through the development of new nations in the present century, especially after World War II. Along with *national* identity in places like Jordan, Morocco, Libya, Algeria, Pakistan, Indonesia, Malaysia, and other countries being *Muslim* has also been of critical importance, with different styles and intensity of application in different places. Thus, Pakistan was founded in 1947 as an Islamic state, and Islam has continued to be the most important principle in the development of that nation's institutions. Indonesia, 90 percent Muslim, nevertheless achieved independence from the Netherlands after World War II through an independence movement that carefully balanced religious, nationalistic, and ethnic issues in a pluralistic manner. It was decided that the Republic of Indonesia should be composed of citizens who believe in the one true God, but although the Muslims enjoy a vast majority, the monotheistic traditions of Buddhism (according to the Indonesian interpretation), Hinduism, and Christianity should be included fully in the national idea too. Even so, there has continued in Indonesia a strong Muslim sentiment among many to require the Muslims to be ruled by the *Sharī'a*.

The recent Islamic revolution in Iran, characterized by powerful Shī'ite convictions, considers itself to be returning its people to a sort of divine right rule of the religious scholars, who in Iran are known as *mullas* as well as *'ulamā'*. Although Shī'ites and Sunnīs have long been at odds with each other, they also realize their common Islamic roots and shared beliefs and rituals. They are, in fact, much closer in these and other respects than Protestants and Catholics are within Christianity. The Iranian leaders, especially the Ayatollah Khomeini, preach Islamic unity and condemn sectarian differences and disagreements as fatal in the continuing struggle to preserve Islam from infidel Western ways and to extend the borders of the Islamic community through missionary efforts.

Islamic revivalist strength in many places does not mean that there is a coordinated monolithic organization and structure. The tendency of Muslims to take strength from each other and to close ranks for the common good is as old as the religion. The high level of uniformity in worship and social regulations without clerical class or hierarchical government is a product of profound convictions and throughly ingrained spiritual, social, political, and cultural habits. The influence of Qur'ān and Sunna and their proper interpretation and application through legal schools, both in Sunnī and Shī'ite Islam, is at bottom what makes Muslim unity and group loyalty strong. The great variety and wide geographic distribution of Muslim peoples is proof of the religion's appeal and ability to accommodate many different cultures into its vision of faith and order. A monolithic system never could have had such success in winning the allegiance of so many peoples, most of whom had no previous close relations with each other or reason to develop a shared identity at the religious level.

The American anthropologist Clifford Geertz has studied Islam and Muslims in two highly contrasting geographical and cultural contexts, Morocco and Indonesia. The title of his book, *Islam Observed*,[8] is meaningful. Geertz realizes that it is very difficult to define Islam as a social and cultural reality, because of the great differences that exist in different regions at the levels of symbols, folk behavior, historical traditions, and general religious temperament. Moroccans are vigorously competitive, intensely motivated people with a rugged desert and mountain heritage, strongly influenced by Arabism, which arrived early in Islamic history. They possess a narrow scope as a cultural tradition in which Islamic faith and observance combine forcefully with native Moroccan social relations—especially the tribal structure of authority and prestige—to exert a definitive, regulating influence on life. Indonesia, on the other hand, has a very wide cultural scope with tolerant and syncretistic habits, which thus decrease the force of purely Islamic ideals. Old Javanese, Hindu, and Buddhist symbols and customs continue to exert gentle but firm influences, to the extent that stricter Muslims from outside— fundamentalists of the Wahhābi type especially—are often critical of Indonesian Muslims for accommodating so much that is considered un-Islamic by a strict *Sharī'a* attitude. But Indonesian Muslims defend their own ways, and insist that regional customs, known as *adat*, are fully acceptable in combination with scripturally based Islamic values, attitudes, and practices.

Geertz's challenging comparative analysis is a warning against trying to understand a religious tradition as old and broad as Islam by applying book definitions and categories. This viewpoint underlies the title, "Islam Observed." The author does not attempt to *define* Islam before examining it as a complete cultural system in the two countries. Rather, he wants the data to be drawn out and then carefully studied in their proper contexts, before raising the question of what constitutes "Islam" and what lies outside that category. In general, Geertz holds that if people call themselves Muslim, it is then up to the investigator to discern and understand what that may mean in any situation. It is sometimes a complex task, especially when Muslims themselves can be divided on the question, as when theological definitions—based on Scripture and traditional authoritative positions—are invoked.

"Islamic" and "Muslim"

Mohammad Koesnoe, a leading Indonesian specialist on the relationship between Islam and regional folk law (*adat*), distinguishes the terms "Islamic" and "Muslim" when referring to different aspects of Indonesian religious life.[9] "Islamic," for Koesnoe, means that which is based on the Qur'ān and Sunna as interpreted by the major schools of jurisprudence (*fiqh*). More often than not, it is an ideal more than a reality. "Muslim," on the other hand, means that which is produced essentially by human intellect and is therefore subject to critical rational investigation and alteration, if necessary. Koesnoe holds that much of what people call "Islamic" is really just "Muslim," in that it does not have the authority of the Scriptural bases of the religion, but only human consensus and provisional utility backing it up. Koesnoe further contends that even jurisprudence is essentially Muslim rather than Islamic and is thus subject to continual evaluation, reexamination, and improvement. This position allows for considerable flexibility in determining how Muslims may relate the enduring sources of their religious doctrines and laws to actual situations in a historically dynamic world. Koesnoe's position, obviously, favors continual independent legal decision making (*ijtihād*).

Conclusion

Muslims are enjoying greater global unity and accord than have been possible in recent centuries, even though they lament serious divisions and difficulties that plague the *Umma*, such as the Iran-Iraq war, challenges to certain regimes (for example, those in Egypt and Saudi Arabia) by militant and extremist Muslim groups, and sectarian strife such as erupts often in Syria and Lebanon between Shī'ites and Sunnīs. But the overall picture is one of progress, with successes in missionary work, charitable endeavors on the part of the wealthier Islamic nations for those less fortunate, and a regained sense of pride and strength that has largely replaced the feelings of weakness, backwardness, and humiliation of the colonial period. As was remarked early in this chapter, however, there are still problems concerning how Muslims view the Western scientific and technological world, among which is a feeling of being in a neocolonial situation.

One of the most noteworthy aspects of contemporary Islam, as was noted, is its increasing presence in Western countries: Europe, the Americas (especially the United States and Canada), and Australia. Christianity, the dominant religion of the West and of the former colonial powers, never became securely established in Muslim countries except the Balkans and Spain—where it was a matter of reconquest in the presence of a large continuing Christian population—and certain African countries where both religions have often competed openly for converts. Christianity, since the rise of Islam, has not been successful, in spite of sporadic, sometimes intense, attempts at missionary activity, in becoming widespread in the Arabian Peninsula, Turkey, North Africa, Iraq, Iran, Pakistan, Malaysia, or Bangladesh. Until recently, Islam had at most a very weak presence in urban areas of Europe and North America. But now, Islam is enjoying considerable acceptance in these places, so that in some regions, of England and France, for example, the call to prayer can be heard alongside church bells, and the atmosphere of whole neighborhoods is being palpably transformed. Christianity is not making headway in the Islamic world, but Islam is certainly prospering in countries that have a strong tradition of Christian dominance in the religious sphere.

As we observed earlier in this chapter with reference to the Islamic Center of Greater Toledo, as Islam becomes acclimated in the West, especially in North America, it will inevitably take on many aspects of Western culture and society in the process. In an open field for missionary activities, almost anything can happen. Islam's inherent capacity to adapt to and accommodate different cultures and societies, both changing them and being colored by them, is a great advantage in parts of the world that are highly secularized and lukewarm if not indifferent or even hostile to religion. Muslims can freely call their fellow humans to Islam in a great variety of ways, both in strongly Muslim countries and in most other nations as well, especially in the West.

We have included these remarks on Islam in relation to other faiths because the issue is important to Muslims. The Qur'ān itself contains many references to other religious ways, especially Judaism and Christianity, and teaches that Islam is the fulfillment in history and God's plan of both. It is no wonder, then, that Muslims true to their calling should continue to invite others to the Straight Path and to hope for the day when all humans will celebrate together their brother- and sisterhood in a worldwide *Umma*, reflecting God's Unity in human religious unity and harmony, which for Muslims is the culmination of *tawḥīd*, the Divine Unification.

Notes

1. The Islamic Center, Washington, D.C., estimates that there are approximately one billion Muslims in the world, while the 1986 *Encyclopedia Britannica Book of the Year* estimates about 555 million. A region-by-region global survey of Muslim populations is contained in M. Ali Kettani, *Muslim Minorities in the World Today,* Institute of Muslim Minority Affairs, Monograph Series Number 2 (London and New York: Mansell, 1986), which estimates the global Muslim population at approximately one billion thirty million. See the tables on pp. 238–243. Other sources for population statistics of Muslim peoples are *The Statesman's Year-Book,* ed. John Paxton (New York: St. Martin's, 1985–86 and revised annually); *Worldmark Encyclopedia of Nations,* 6th ed., 1984 (New York: Wiley); and United Nations publications. A useful reference work on characteristics of different Muslim societies and regions is Richard V. Weekes, ed., *Muslim Peoples: A World Ethnographic Survey,* 2d rev. ed., 2 vol. (Westport, Conn.: Greenwood, 1984). There are valuable appendices with population estimates for all Muslim ethnic groups.

2. The Muslim calendar is reckoned by the phases of the moon and is divided into twelve months of twenty-nine or thirty days, with a total year of around 354 days. Because of the lunar reckoning, the Muslim year falls behind the solar year by about eleven days annually. The Qur'ān forbids intercalation—adding extra days periodically—to make up for this discrepancy. The Muslim calendar governs religious observances, but most Muslim countries also use the common solar calendar without attaching any spiritual significance to it. Conversion charts are available for comparing Muslim and Western historical dates.

3. I am indebted to Professor Juan Campo, University of California, Santa Barbara, for this interpretation.

4. Translations from the Qur'ān in this section are my own, although I am indebted to the following recommended translations, which have been consulted: A. J. Arberry, *The Koran Interpreted* (New York: Macmillan, 1964); Mohammed Marmaduke Pickthall, *The Meaning of the Glorious Koran* (New York: New American Library and Mentor Books, n.d.); and A. Yusuf Ali, *The Holy Qur'ān* (1934; various reprintings).

5. *Ṣaḥīḥ Muslim,* (Beirut: Dār al-Fikr, 1398/1978), I:282, no. 116. (An English translation of Muslim by Abdul Hamid Siddiqi has been published in 4 vol. by Sh. Muhammad Ashraf, Lahore, Pakistan, 1976.)

6. As quoted in A. J. Arberry, *Sufism* (New York: Harper & Row, Torchbooks, 1970), p. 28.

7. Reynold A. Nicholson, trans., *Rūmī: Poet and Mystic, 1207–1273* (London: Allen and Unwin, 1950), pp. 122–123

8. Clifford Geertz, *Islam Observed: Religious Development in Morocco and Indonesia* (New Haven: Yale University Press, 1968).

9. Professor Koesnoe outlined his views in a series of class lectures in the Department of Religious Studies, University of Colorado, Boulder, Spring Semester 1986.

Glossary

'Abbāsid. Muslim dynasty (750–1258 C.E.) centered in Iraq (Baghdad) under which Islamic civilization achieved maturity.

Allāh. Arabic word for "God," lit., *al-ilāh,* "the god."

baraka. "Blessing" or "spiritual power" believed to reside in holy places and persons.

Basmala. The name for the sacred Islamic invocation "In the Name of God, the Merciful, the Compassionate" (*bi'smillāh al-raḥmān al-raḥīm*) uttered frequently by pious Muslims, as before meals, before writing something down or making a speech, before conjugal relations, before reciting the Qur'ān, and at other times.

bid'a. Lit., "innovation," but a term that came to mean "heresy."

caliph. Lit., "successor," "deputy," "vicegerent"; in the Qur'ān it refers to people who submit in voluntary service to God and are thus empowered to carry on a free and active life as God's vicegerents on earth; in the early history of Islam, caliph is the title for the military/political leaders of the *Umma* functioning as Muhammad's "successor" in all but the prophetic role.

Dār al-Islām. "The Household of Submission," meaning the territories governed by Muslims under the *Sharī'a;* the term's opposite is *Dār al-Ḥarb,* "The Household of Warfare," those lands lacking the security and guidance of God's law.

da'wa. The "calling" of people to the religion of Islam; thus, "missions."

dhikr. "Remembering," "mentioning" God by means of his names and his words in the Qur'ān, the central practice of Sufi meditation.

fiqh. Lit., "understanding" in matters of religious law; Islamic jurisprudence.

fiṭra. The original framework or nature of humans as created by God, considered good.

fundamentalism. A term originally applied to conservative Protestant Christians, but more recently applied to religiously conservative Muslims who interpret their Scriptures literally and in general favor a strict adherence to their doctrines and practices.

ḥadīth. "Report," or "account," a tradition about Muḥammad—what he said or did on a particular occasion; the *ḥadīths* were collected and they came to be a record of the Prophet's Sunna, which is second only to the Qur'ān in authority for Muslims.

Ḥajj. The pilgrimage to Mecca and one of the five Pillars of Islam.

ḥanīf. Pre-Islamic Arabian monotheists whose beliefs are thought to have descended from the time of Abraham.

Hijra. The "emigration" of Muhammad and the Muslims from Mecca to Medina in 622 C.E.; the Muslim lunar calendar dates from that year.

'Ibāda. "Service" to God through worship by means of the five Pillars.

iḥrām. The state of ritual purity and dedication entered into by the pilgrim on *Ḥajj* to Mecca.

ijmā'. "Consensus," one of the four sources of Sunni jurisprudence.

ijtihād. Intellectual "effort" of Muslim jurists to reach independent religio-legal decisions, a key feature of modern Islamic reform; one who exercises *ijtihād* is a *mujtahid.*

imām. "Leader," specifically of the *Ṣalāt* prayer service; in Shī'ite Islam, *imām* also refers to one of the revered early leaders of the community who both ruled in the political sense and also interpreted doctrine with infallible, God-given wisdom.

īmān. "Faith"; one who has faith is a *mu'min,* "believer."

Islām. "Submission" to God, the name of the true religion, according to the Qur'ān; one who submits is a Muslim.

Jāhilīya. The pre-Islamic Arabian age of "ignorance," marked by barbarism and unbelief; Islam came to end this evil age, according to its view.

jihād. "Exertion" in the work of God, including, sometimes, armed force.

Ka'ba. The sacred cubical shrine in Mecca, toward which Muslims face in prayer; legend says the *Ka'ba* was built by Abraham.

Karbalā'. The place in Iraq where Ḥusayn, grandson of Muḥammad and son of 'Alī and Fāṭima, was ambushed and killed on his way to assume leadership over the Shī'ites in Iraq, a tragic event commemorated each year on the tenth of the Muslim month of Muḥarram.

kiai. An Indonesian term for a religious teacher of high status.

maḥram. The bounds of close blood relationship within which it is unlawful to marry and thus lawful for members of the opposite sex to associate socially (as between brothers and sisters, aunts and nephews, and so forth.)

mawlid. "Birthday" celebration, most often used in connection with Muḥammad and the saints of Islam.

mosque. English corruption of the Arabic word *masjid,* "place of prostration" for performing the *Ṣalāt.*

Muhammadiyah. Twentieth-century Indonesian Islamic reform movement emphasizing purity of faith and practices and service to fellow Muslims, especially through education.

Muslim. One who has submitted to God by Islam, lit., "submitter."

Pillars of Islam. The five basic devotional-ritual duties of Islam: *Shahāda,* testifying that "There is no god but God, and Muḥammad is the Messenger of God"; *Ṣalāt,* five daily prayer services; *Zakāt,* almsgiving; *Ṣawm,* fasting during daylight in the month of Ramaḍān; *Ḥajj,* pilgrimage to Mecca.

pondok pesantren. An Islamic boarding school in Indonesia with a traditional curriculum based on the Qur'ān.

Qur'ān. Lit., "recitation," the Islamic Scripture, believed to have been revealed to Muḥammad orally through the angel Gabriel.

Quraysh. The leading Meccan tribe to which Muḥammad belonged.

Ramaḍān. The holy month of fasting, during which the Qur'ān was first revealed.

sakīna. A divine "tranquility" that is believed to descend when the Qur'ān is recited.

Ṣalāt. The obligatory Muslim prayer service held five times daily, one of the Pillars of Islam.

Ṣawm. "Fasting" during the month of Ramaḍān, one of the Pillars of Islam.

sayyid. A title borne by descendants of the Prophet Muḥammad.

Shahāda. Lit., "witnessing" that "There is no god but God, Muḥammad is the Messenger of God," a kind of minimal creed for Muslims and one of the Pillars of Islam.

Sharī'a. The "Way" of Islam, including law and governance, according to the Qur'ān and Sunna.

shaykh. Arabic word meaning an old man with grey hairs, a term that came to mean a respected leader and in Islam a religious teacher or person learned in religion or respected for piety.

Shī'a. Lit., "party," of 'Alī; the Shī'ites believe that Muḥammad designated his son-in-law, 'Alī, to succeed him as leader of the *Umma* of Islam; the Shī'ite community numbers up to 20 percent of the total Muslim community today.

shirk. "Association" of something with God, thus "idolatry," the one unforgiveable sin according to the Qur'ān.

Sufism. The mystical path of Islam.

Sunna. The "custom" of the Prophet Muḥammad, that is, his words, habits, acts, and gestures as remembered by the Muslims and preserved in the literary form of the *ḥadīth* reports. The Sunna is second only to the Qur'ān in authority for Muslims.

Sunnīs. The majority of Muslims, who believe that any good Muslim can be leader; they prefer to reach agreements by means of consensus and do not recognize special sacred wisdom in their leaders as Shī'ites do.

sūra. A chapter of the Qur'ān, of which there are 114 in all.

tafsīr. Interpretation of the Qur'ān, of which there are various types.

taqlīd. Adoption and imitation of traditional legal decisions. Criticized by reform-minded legal thinkers as blind imitation—the opposite of *ijtihād.*

Ṭarīqa. Lit., "way" of Sufism as a whole as the mystical path of Islam in contrast to the *Sharī'a,* the religious law; *ṭarīqa* also refers to a specific Sufi organization or method of meditation.

tawḥīd. The divine unity, Islam's central doctrine.

ta'zīya. Lit., "consolation"; a Shī'ite passion play commemorating the tragic death of the third Imām, *Ḥusayn,* at Karbalā', in 680 C.E.

tilāwa. Ritual recitation of the Qur'ān.

'ulamā'. Scholars "learned" in Islamic law, the top class of religious officials in Islam.

Umma. The Muslim "community" worldwide.

Wahhābis. Puritanical Muslim reform movement that arose in Arabia in the eighteenth century under Muḥammad ibn 'Abd al-Wahhāb (1703–1787).

waḥy. "Revelation" of the Qur'ān to Muḥammad by a kind of verbal/mental process of inspiration.

walī. "Friend," "client," "kinsman," "patron"; in English *walī* most often means Muslim "saint" or "holy person."

Zakāt. Legal almsgiving required as a Pillar of Islam.

Selected Reading List

Abdalati, Hammudah. *Islam in Focus.* Indianapolis, Ind.: Islamic Trust Publications, 1977.

Arberry, A. J., trans. *The Koran Interpreted.* New York: Macmillan, 1964.

Beck, Lois Grant, and Nikkie Keddie, eds. *Women in the Muslim World.* Cambridge, Mass.: Harvard University Press, 1978.

Cragg, Kenneth. *The Event of the Qur'ān: Islam in Its Scripture.* London: Allen & Unwin, 1971.

—, *The Mind of the Qur'ān: Chapters in Reflection.* London: Allen & Unwin, 1973.

Cragg, Kenneth, and R. Marston Speight, eds. *Islam from Within: Anthology of a Religion.* Belmont, Calif.: Wadsworth, 1980. Original sources in translation.

Denny, Frederick Mathewson. *An Introduction to Islam.* New York: Macmillan, 1985.

Denny, Frederick Mathewson, and Abdulaziz A. Sachedina. *Islamic Ritual Practices: A Slide Set and Teacher's Guide.* Asian Religions Media Resources, Vol. 7. New Haven, Conn.: Paul Vieth Christian Education Service, Yale Divinity School, 1983. 180 color slides and 115 p. text.

Encyclopaedia of Islam, New ed. Leiden: Brill, 1954–. An essential reference. An abridgment of the first edition, containing articles on religion only, is *Shorter Encyclopedia of Islam,* ed. H. A. R. Gibb and J. H. Kramers (Leiden: Brill, 1953.) See the Register of Subjects, pp. 663–665, for help in finding technical entry words, most of which are Arabic.

Gätje, Helmut. *The Qur'ān and its Exegesis.* Trans. Alford T. Welch. London: Routledge and Kegan Paul, 1976. Translations of representative *tafsīr* works.

Geertz, Clifford. *Islam Observed: Religious Development in Morocco and Indonesia.* New Haven, Conn.: Yale University Press, 1968. Emphasizes cultural differences.

Gilsenan, Michael. *Recognizing Islam: An Anthropologist's Introduction.*

London and Canberra: Croom and Helm, 1983. Muslims understood by a keen observer.

Guillaume, Alfred, trans. *The Life of Muhammad: A Translation of Isḥāq's Sīrat Rasūl Allāh.* London: Oxford University Press, 1967. The standard early Islamic biography.

Haddad, Yvonne Yazbeck, and Adair T. Lummis. *Islamic Values in the United States.* New York: Oxford University Press, 1987. Important sociological analysis.

Haneef, Suzanne. *What Everyone Should Know About Islam and Muslims.* Chicago: Kazi Publications, 1982. Good overview from a Muslim perspective.

Hodgson, Marshall G. S. *The Venture of Islam: Conscience and History in a World Civilization.* 3 vols. Chicago: University of Chicago Press, 1974.

Lewis, Bernard. *The Arabs in History.* 4th rev. ed. New York: Harper & Row, 1966.

Momen, Moojan. *An Introduction to Shī'ī Islam.* New Haven, Conn. and London: Yale University Press, 1985.

Nasr, Seyyed Hossein. *Ideals and Realities of Islam.* Boston: Beacon Press, 1972.

Pickthall, Mohammed Marmaduke, trans. *The Meaning of the Glorious Koran.* New York: New American Library and Mentor Books, n. d. Muslim-approved translation.

Rahman, Fazlur. *Islam.* 2d ed. Chicago: University of Chicago Press, 1979.

—. *Islam and Modernity: Transformation of an Intellectual Tradition.* Chicago: University of Chicago Press, 1982.

—. *Major Themes of the Qur'ān.* Minneapolis and Chicago: Bibliotheca Islamica, 1980. Important interpretations by a leading contemporary Muslim scholar.

Schacht, Joseph, and C. E. Bosworth, eds. *The Legacy of Islam.* 2d.ed. Oxford: Clarendon Press, 1974. Politics, war, economics, art, architecture, science, law and the state, philosophy and theology, mysticism, literature.

Schimmel, Annemarie. *Mystical Dimensions of Islam.* Chapel Hill, N. C.: The University of North Carolina Press, 1975.

Watt, W. Montgomery. *Bell's Introduction to the Qur'ān.* Edinburgh: Edinburgh University Press, 1970.

—. *The Formative Period of Islamic Thought.* Edinburgh: Edinburgh University Press, 1973.

Weekes, Richard V. ed., *Muslim Peoples: A World Ethnographic Survey,* 2d rev. ed., 2 vol. (Westport, Conn.: Greenwood, 1984). Includes extensive bibliographies.

Wensinck, Arendt Jan. *The Muslim Creed: Its Genesis and Historical Development.* Cambridge: Cambridge University Press, 1932.

PAK = 91 M
BANK = 86 M
IND = 75 M

252

INDON - 150

402